Training Retrievers

The Cotton Pershall Method

Training Retrievers

The Cotton Pershall Method

Bobby N. George, Jr.

Foreword by Michael McIntosh

STACKPOLE
BOOKS
Guilford, Connecticut

Editor's Note

In the thirty years since this book's first edition appeared, Cotton Pershall has followed to his final rest King Buck, Tar of Arden, Shed of Arden, and the many other wonderful dogs that he trained during his half-century career. Although the sporting world has lost, arguably, its greatest retriever trainer, Pershall's legacy lives on through Bobby George's systematic presentation of his training methods. Throughout the preparation of this new printing of George's book, we have kept in mind the admonishment, "If it ain't broke, don't fix it." Thus, from the Foreword to the Glossary of Terms, *Training Retrievers: The Cotton Pershall Method* remains as originally written—including anecdotal references to Cotton in the present tense—by the unique collaboration of George and Pershall.

Published by Stackpole Books
An imprint of The Rowman & Littlefield Publishing Group, Inc.
4501 Forbes Blvd., Ste. 200
Lanham, MD 20706
www.rowman.com

Distributed by NATIONAL BOOK NETWORK

Copyright © 1990 by Bobby N. George, Jr.
Reprint edition 2005
First Stackpole Books paperback edition 2021

British Library Cataloguing in Publication Information available

Library of Congress Cataloging-in-Publication Data available

ISBN 978-0-8927-2699-8 (cloth: alk. paper)
ISBN 978-0-8117-3999-3 (paper: alk. paper)
ISBN 978-0-8117-6985-3 (electronic)

∞™ The paper used in this publication meets the minimum requirements of American National Standard for Information Sciences—Permanence of Paper for Printed Library Materials, ANSI/NISO Z39.48-1992.

ACKNOWLEDGEMENTS

Changes in dog training techniques and equipment have been dramatic since the first edition of this book was published in 1990.

However, now as then, there is no substitute, no gadget, no "new" theory to take the place of the hard work and the instincts of the dedicated dog man. He is passion driven, he respects the creatures he trains, he exercises patience, and he develops the intuition and insight to get into a dog's head and know what the dog is going to do before he does it.

Cotton Pershall was such a man—a true dog man. He would excel today the way he excelled in midcentury. He was a great teacher of both dogs and people. Thanks Cotton, for setting the standard.

As this is being written, the best dog man in the country, Bill Eckett, and his wife Becky are driving home from the National Open Retriever Championship in Texas. He is my friend and mentor and is bringing home the winner's trophy. Thanks Bill and Becky, for letting me be a part of the Blackwater Retrievers team. Thanks, too, for maintaining the standard.

Thanks also go to all the road pros, those gypsies who travel the interstates and back roads in their stainless steel carnival rigs full of great dogs. Drive safely brothers.

Then there is Suzy. She keeps the standard alive by keeping the trainer alive. She's been with me through the storms, the mud, the barking dogs, and the winter trips. She hangs tough, a big part in maintaining the standard.

Finally, I want to acknowledge Beve Lincoln and FC-AFC Links Royal Touch of Class. The lady and the Lab who set a standard for living, for conduct, style, and common decency toward which all of us should strive.

CONTENTS

CONTENTS

vii

FOREWORD

Odd, you might suppose, that a gun writer should introduce a book on dog training. Maybe so, but for the moment I'm speaking as someone who has carried on a lifelong love affair with dogs, as someone utterly charmed by the nature of dogs, intensely interested in canine psychology, and in the nearly primal relationship between dogs and men.

Consequently, I'm speaking as one who holds some strong opinions on dogs and the training thereof, most of which I won't inflict upon you in any detail. But I also hold some equally strong opinions on Cotton Pershall and Bobby George, and whatever the feelings may be worth, you ought to know a few of the facts.

Cotton and I first crossed paths years ago, when he was chief trainer at Nilo Kennels. It was a chance meeting, one of literally thousands in Cotton's life and, on his part, easily forgotten. There was no reason why he should remember a little-known writer, but neither I nor anyone else interested in dogs could forget Cotton Pershall. I could spin out a catalogue of his accomplishments from now 'til duck season, but I can just as easily boil it all down to one word.

Legend.

It's like this: If the task is to induce a dog to willingly perform a prescribed set of behaviors, Cotton Pershall can do it. If the methodology is intelligent, imaginative, effective, reliable, and sound, Cotton Pershall either invented or refined it.

Legend.

Cotton's retired from Nilo now and lives just a few miles down the road from where I live. He still trains dogs, of course, but perhaps more important, he trains trainers. Stop by the farm almost any day, and you'll probably find Cotton guiding two or three young dogs through land patterns in the pasture or doing some water work at one of the ponds. Likely as not, there'll be a young man there with him, someone with a taste for retriever trials or gun dogs, someone who has come to learn from The Master.

My friend Bobby George has spent a lot of time at Cotton's place, talking, training, working, and learning. As a result, you now have in your hands something unique.

Dog-training books have been written by charlatans, bozos, and clods, and their existence has all too often been to the detriment of dogs and the confusion of those who own them. Some astonishingly famous and unfortunately durable books have been written from the author's experience with only a single dog. Others dangle the specious promise that successful dog training can be an effortless exercise requiring no more than a few minutes of attention whenever you happen to have the time and inclination.

So you don't have to look far to find bad training books well written or good methods poorly presented. You won't find any such nonsense here.

Cotton Pershall and Bobby George are the real quill, and together they've come up with gem of a book. Besides being a first-class writer, Bobby is himself a thoughtful dog trainer of considerable skill. What you'll find in these pages amounts to a complete training method, The Cotton Pershall Method, if you will, systematically set down in print for the first time.

There's something here for every level of experience among dogs and trainers alike, and there are two things you can count on: Any technique that Cotton recommends has been tested and honed through thousands of hours spent working with untold hundreds of dogs. Moreover, you'll find it all organized and presented at a level of clarity and sheer good writing that any book would be proud to own.

In practical terms, how much you get out of it will depend upon how much you put in – how much time and thought, patience and sensitivity, love and dedication. Those qualities and this book are all the tools you need.

Chances are, you already know where to find a willing student.

MICHAEL MCINTOSH
Jefferson City, Missouri

THEODORE W. 'COTTON' PERSHALL: AN INTRODUCTION

Theodore W. 'Cotton' Pershall did not learn to train retrievers from a book.

In a crowd of professional retriever trainers, Cotton would probably be the first to stand up and say it can't be done. Train a retriever by reading a book, that is.

As usual, Cotton is right.

Retrievers, unlike bicycles and prefab bookcases, don't come with assembly directions. Even if they did, major pieces are often missing.

Most retriever training, good retriever training, comes from the gut. Something inside, the dregs of an ancient instinct maybe, flips the switches.

Experience plays a big part, of course. The more dogs you can work with, the quicker you will develop the proper training reactions and the better you will become at understanding some of the things dogs do.

Ron Batman, a member of the Kansas City Retriever Club, succinctly described trainer reactions one morning while we were shooting pigeons at a "fun" trial. He said there are good trainers and great trainers. A good trainer, he said, watches a dog work and when the dog makes a mistake or otherwise gets himself in a position for an effective correction, the good trainer reacts. And, most of the time, he reacts with the right correction.

The great trainer, he said, knows what the dog is going to do before he does it. He doesn't have to make the correct, split-second decision because he knows what is going to happen. Great trainers, he said, *know* – like D.L. Walters – and Cotton Pershall.

Not long after this conversation, Cotton punctuated Batman's evaluation with one of his psychic-like observations. I was at a field trial in St. Louis when a friend of Cotton's came off the line with her dog. She was beaming. It was the last series of the qualifying and her dog had done well. Her greeting was lost in his scowl.

"Trained in corn stubble this week, didn't you?" he said. Puzzled, she said that, yes, they had run a couple of days in corn stubble to prepare for the trial. "How," she asked, "did you know?"

"I could tell the way he was running! Working in corn stubble makes 'em sore in the shoulders. Slows 'em down. Hell, that dog's all bound up in the shoulders."

No one – not the dog's owner, nor any of her training group – had noticed.

I have grown to expect this type of Holmesian deduction from the man.

I met Cotton in 1985. Actually, I *imposed* myself on Cotton in 1985. I had heard at a field trial that he lived in Eldon, Missouri, so I called directory assistance the following week just on the chance that he would be listed. He was. The subsequent phone call resulted in an invitation to "come on down." The next Saturday Jerel Scott, a fellow field trialer and duck hunter, and I found ourselves parked in the middle of a gravel road staring at a mailbox that read "T.W. Pershall." The emotion was similar to that of a 12-year-old kid standing outside a locker room, knowing that Babe Ruth would be strolling by at any moment.

Neither one of us had the nerve to bring a dog, which Cotton couldn't understand. The next weekend, when we did bring our dogs, he understood why we left them home a lot. But, with Cotton's help, we eventually turned even those two potlickers into passable gun dogs.

Making decent dogs out of marginal dogs is a pretty ordinary feat for Cotton. But the things he could do with truly good dogs was extraordinary.

Cotton's life changed dramatically at the ripe old age of 13. A barefooted country boy from Walnut Ridge, Arkansas, he moved to St. Louis where he had been hired to work with the horses owned by Paul Bakewell III. Cotton's formal education ended there. But it was only the beginning of what he was to learn.

Paul Bakewell III was Cotton's first employer in the dog game. Together the two men set a torrid pace for those who would compete in retriever field trials. This photo of Bakewell was made November 2, 1947 at Westhampton Beach, Long Island. Alongside Bakewell is Dual Champion Little Pierre of Deer Creek.

In the 1930's, Bakewell, whose family fortune sprang from the insurance business, joined many of the nation's wealthy in a new sport – retriever field trials. Bakewell soon slanted Cotton toward dog training, and the two learned the game together – not from books, but from trial and error.

Cotton said about that time a Scotsman, Dave Elliott, brought "handling" to the United States. He was the first to teach retrievers to take whistle commands and hand signals. Elliott was the father of the handling retriever, and the young Cotton Pershall soon became the father of the "lining" retriever.

The concept of lining came to him on a bridle trail in St. Louis. He said while walking a dog down one of the many bridle trails near

Cotton receives Bracken's Sweep during the 1947 National Championship Stake at Herrin, Illinois. Bracken's Sweep went on to win the event, one of three Cotton Pershall-trained retrievers that won five national championships during the 1940s.

Bakewell's stable, he dropped bumpers behind him, aimed more at playing with the dog than teaching him anything. After he had dropped a half-dozen bumpers or so, he stopped, turned the dog to face in the direction they had come, and sent him for one bumper after another. Teaching a dog to "take a line" had begun. Similar training drills are still in use today.

While with Bakewell, Cotton trained Rip, the first golden retriever to win an open field trial stake. He also trained Tar of Arden and Shed of Arden, the latter a three-time national champion. Still in the 40's, he trained and handled Bracken's Sweep, the 1947 national champion, and Marvadel Black Gum, the 1949 national champion. The *Field & Stream* Trophy was awarded during this period to the high-point field trial retriever of the year. Rip won it in 1939 and '40; Tar in '41; Shed in '42, '43, and '46; Bracken's Sweep in '47; and Marvadel Black Gum in '49. Cotton pointed out that while he did the bulk of the training with Shed, Bakewell did the handling in the national stakes.

Cotton left Bakewell and joined John Olin and Nilo Kennels in 1951. Cotton trained dogs at Nilo (Olin spelled backward) until his retirement in 1982.

He kicked off the golden years of the retriever field trail game in 1952 by winning the national retriever championship with King Buck. He repeated the triumph in 1953. In Buck's field trial career, he completed 83 national open championship series out of a possible 85. No retriever has equaled this feat. In 1959, Buck was immortalized on the Federal Duck Stamp, the only retriever ever to hold this honor.

Cotton's voice takes on a deeper timbre when he speaks of Buck.

King Buck delivers a mallard to Cotton during the 1952 National Championship Stake at the August A. Busch Memorial Wildlife Area near Weldon Springs, Missouri. Buck won the stake, adding yet another national championship to Cotton's long string of victories.

King Buck did it again in 1953 – back-to-back national championships! John Olin, Cotton and Buck share the limelight at the end of the four-day trial held November 19 – 22 at Easton, Maryland.

King Buck delivers gently to hand during the 1953 National Championship Stake. In Buck's career, he completed 83 national open championship series out of a possible 85.

Their relationship went to the heart.

"I ain't seen a dog that could even smell where he's been," Cotton said. "Linin', handlin', runnin', or doin' anything else."

Cotton has a thousand stories about Buck. But the only story I have heard him tell just once dealt with Buck's last days.

"I didn't get Mr. Olin's opinion," Cotton said as we sat at his kitchen table. "He didn't want to know about it. Buck's eyes were cloudy a little bit, but he wasn't blind. He was put down about four days before his birthday in 1962. He had arthritis and he was gettin' dehydrated. You could see him shrinking, and it was gettin' kind of hard for him to get up in his dog house. I just wasn't going to see the dog in that kind of shape. I had the vet do it. He was at Nilo when he was put down – buried at Nilo, and there's a cast aluminum sculpture of Buck that marks his grave right by the kennel house. Every year it gets a fresh coat of black paint. Mr. Olin just didn't want to hear anything about it."

The story about Buck surviving an early bout with distemper is

16

common knowledge among old-time field trialers. Maybe not so common knowledge is that Buck, one of the all-time great retrievers, and Cotton, one of the all-time great retriever trainers, share the same birthday – April 3. Maybe the stars do hold the secrets of our fates.

Cotton made 28 field champions, more than one a year during his active career, and he won three national open titles while he was at Nilo. The third win came in 1965 with Martens Little Smoky. Cotton retired from field trialing in 1975. He still has 11 dogs ranked in the top 200 high-scoring field trial retrievers of all time, according to the latest statistics of *Retriever Field Trial News*.

Cotton has always been looked upon as a dog guru and Nilo as a kind of retriever-training temple. Myths abound. Some pros still believe that Cotton gave every dog in the kennel a flyer pheasant every day. Of course, the expense would have been astronomical.

Cotton said his dogs didn't get a pheasant every day, but he added, it didn't hurt for people to believe that kind of thing. Anyway, some days they shot ducks for the dogs.

Cotton poses with his last national champion, Martens Little Smoky. The two teamed up to win the 1965 National Championship Stake at the Bombay Hook National Wildlife Refuge near Smyrna, Delaware.

Theodore W. "Cotton" Pershall. After 50 years, he's still training dogs – and training trainers. (A. John Baker Photo)

Cotton's professional accomplishments are unequaled by anyone in the retriever business, but put his professional achievements aside, and Cotton is still one of the true characters I have ever met. In a society where most people try their damndest to fit neatly into specific marketing categories, Cotton's an original.

He is not formally educated, yet those who are come to him to learn. He is a down-home country boy, yet he talks of business trips to England with John Olin as if they were trips around the block. He is proud of his accomplishments and lets you know it, but he is humble enough to stand on a levee in driving rain to help you teach a hopelessly inept dog a simple water mark. If Cotton had chosen the stock market for a career instead of dog training, there would probably be a street in New York City called Pershall Boulevard.

There is only one facet of retriever training from which Cotton shied – the electronic collar. In Cotton's heyday, "collar" training was not as sophisticated as it is today. It was used, for the most part, like an electronic shotgun. When the dog was 150 yards away and wouldn't sit on the whistle, he got licked with electricity. The collar is used differently today, more scientifically.

Cotton, on the other hand, used a shotgun for correcting his field trial dogs. There has never been anyone better at this type of correction than Cotton. His judgment, to this day, is impeccable. He never shoots at a dog in anger and his ability to quickly estimate range is amazing. He manages to always wait until a dog is far enough away that the gun will not inflict a wound, but the dog will still understand the message provided by a good "dusting."

This book does not deal with such corrections. These are both tools of the professional trainer and require a great deal of experience to be used effectively. For the most part, they are field trial trainer's tools, necessary to hone a dog to complete the demanding tests seen in trials today.

The shotgun, as you might imagine, is swiftly losing ground to the electronic collar in the retriever business. There are still "conventional" trainers in operation, but realistically speaking, their days are numbered.

Cotton bemoans the advances, claiming that the collar saps the dog of style – the tail-flagging, high-rolling gait of the classic American retriever. Cotton says "collar trainers" turn too many good dogs into pigs.

The winner of both the 1987 U.S. National Open Championship and the 1988 Canadian National Open Championship, Bill Eckett of Blackwater Retrievers, a collar trainer, feels that the great trainers of the past actually created today's training attitudes and methods. They are the reason the sport has reached such a sophisticated level, Bill said. Trainers like Cotton were so good, their dogs so well-trained, that nobody could beat them. Eventually the collar, and its effective use to change behavior, enabled others to compete.

Bill stressed that this was in no way an insult to men like Cotton; rather, it was a compliment.

The objective of this book is to give the would-be trainer a simple program by which a dog can be trained to a relatively high level of competency. There are no deadlines included here, and you can start a puppy with this program or you can start a year-old dog; the latter will just require more muscle and more patience.

You must remember that some retrievers will perform certain phases of this program better than others. Dogs, like people, have weaknesses and strengths. Work on the weaknesses and maintain the strengths.

As you progress through the program, you'll find that Cotton and I have tried to describe a few of the problems you might see and how to fix them. By no means are these all the problems, which means you will have to use your better judgment at times to get past undetermined problems that crop up with your dog. When in doubt, fall back on simplicity. Ask yourself how to simplify the particular step being taught, how to break the lesson down into its simplest elements. Like Cotton says, sometimes you've got to be smarter than the dog.

It is most important, as you progress in the program, to be thorough. If you are proceeding too fast, the dog will become confused. If this happens, drop back a couple of steps and make sure the dog understands the simpler elements before you proceed. Making a good retriever is like making a good football player. The fundamentals – those ho-hum fundamentals – are essential.

In discussing training problems recently with a professional gun dog trainer in Nebraska, he alluded to those "damn training books." He said owners invariably bring him dogs with problems generated from these books. He said most of the time he can find the specific chapter where the problems occurred. We have tried to short-circuit as many problems as we can with this book. But if you run into an insurmountable training obstacle, call a professional trainer for help.

Earlier, I wrote that Cotton would be the first to say that you couldn't train a dog by reading a book. Cotton will tell you that dog training is 99 percent hard work and persistence.

This book was written to provide that missing one percent.

The inspiration.

The rest is up to you.

Cotton begins the day's training with that familiar grin and a story-laden lecture. (Michael McIntosh Photo)

Chapter One

THE TRAINER:
READING
AND
UNDERSTANDING
THE RETRIEVER

Cotton leaned forward, his hands holding the edge of the kitchen table. There was that familiar grin, thin lips parted slightly.

"Tar of Arden was the greatest Labrador bitch that ever lived," he said. "But even she had problems."

He took a sip from his bottomless glass of Pepsi and began.

"It was right after I came back from the war (World War II). I was working for Bakewell at the time and when I got back, Tar was working her birds over pretty bad. Now this was a fine bitch when I left for the service. She was just as gentle...anyway, I talked to the fellows who had been workin' for Bakewell with the dogs while I was gone and no one could explain it.

"Everyone said it had cropped up overnight, a mystery. I mean she was crunchin' bones in her birds!

"One day I just happened to be talking to one of the kennel boys and something was said about Tar and he said, 'She is one good dog, Mr. Pershall.' I said, 'Now what makes you say that?' He said, 'Well, Mr. Pershall, we been havin' her kill the rats down at the stables and she's real good at it. She chases 'em down and

23

grabs 'em and just shakes 'em til they're dead.'

"Well, I tried everything to break her of that habit with the birds and never did get her back to the way she was before I left for the war."

The point?

Retrievers, even great retrievers, learn bad habits just as quickly as they learn good habits. They are creatures of opportunity. Generally speaking, they will take what they perceive to be the easiest way out of any situation. The person who hopes to train a retriever to a finished level must keep this in mind.

Retrievers have been compared to children in the way they learn. The comparison is real, but never believe that the dog actually thinks in human terms. Don't think that big black dog in the kennel behind the house couldn't survive without his expensive, scientifically formulated dog food. As a matter of fact, most retrievers, like all the hunting breeds, are only slightly removed from their wild counterparts.

The "right decision" to a retriever is generally that decision which feels good or is the most convenient. So it is the trainer's job to teach the dog that what feels good is that which pleases the trainer. During puppyhood, training can be accomplished with only small doses of pressure. This saves time and energy later, when the pup has grown to 90 pounds and could pull a car if the roading harness would stand the strain.

Cotton admits that while an old dog *can* learn new tricks, the methods become increasingly severe as the dog gets older. He also points out that good habits painstakingly taught to a puppy through patient repetition can fade quickly if those same habits are not reinforced later in the dog's life.

"You've got to get the dog's respect," Cotton said. "And to do that you've got to earn it. Affection is fine. Pettin' and praisin' are nice. But if you put the pressure on them, they'll have respect for you. (At Nilo Farms) The boys would feed my dogs and everything and then they'd let 'em out of the kennels and exercise 'em. And if they'd see me, they'd leave the kennel boys like a hot potato – zoom! The boys would be hollerin' and those dogs wouldn't pay any attention to 'em. They'd come to me, because I was the one who disciplined them."

The trainer has to be a consistent disciplinarian. "Sit" means put that tail on the ground whether the dog is standing at the kitchen door waiting to go outside or whether he is standing on the bow of a duck boat as 40 mallards circle the decoys.

But the prospective trainer also must realize that there are no absolutes in dealing with retrievers. There can be no guarantees when it comes to training. The dog is not, and can never be, a machine. At the same time, retriever training is forever. The dog never reaches a point where he doesn't need to be trained. Think of retriever training like coaching an athlete. If a sub-four-minute miler goes without training for a month, he is no longer going to be a sub-four-minute miler. The same goes for retrievers. Don't expect a dog to be a pinpoint marker if he gets out of his kennel only on Sunday afternoon for a romp in the park.

But even if you train religiously, everyday, never say "never."

"I've had people tell me their dog would never break on shot," Cotton said, teeth peeking through that grin. "Well, there is no such thing as 'never.' That is, if the dog is any good. The steadiest dog is gonna break now and then when the conditions are right.

"I remember in 1952, after King Buck won his first national championship, Mr. Olin loaded him on an airplane just a couple of hours after the trial was over and flew him to Stuttgart, Arkansas. They were going duck hunting for a few days. Buck would go down there and Mr. Olin would let him sleep on the bed and I don't know what all.

"Anyway, as they were leaving, I told Mr. Olin not to let Buck break. About a week later, I talked to Mr. Olin and asked him if he had any problems with Buck, if Buck had broke on him or anything.

"Mr. Olin said, 'Oh, he broke a couple of times, but don't worry about it Cotton, he'll be all right.' Shoot, it always took me a couple

Less than 24 hours after Paul Bakewell III (center) had offered his congratulations for Buck's victory at the 1952 National Championship Stake, Buck and his master John Olin (right), were sitting in a duck blind near Stuttgart, Arkansas.

of weeks to get him steadied up again after one of those trips.

"I'll tell you what, though, I've trained a few dogs I wish would've broke. A dog that breaks now and then usually has a lot of desire. A dog that doesn't, that kind of watches the birds go down and doesn't have much desire when it comes to retrieving, is not pleasurable to hunt with – at least not to me."

Desire. It is the single most important quality a retriever can possess. Desire will keep him going from the time he is a seven-week-old puppy until his last limping steps to the duck blind. And don't think that just because you have an American Kennel Club registered retriever that the dog is going to be a fine duck dog. Given just about any litter of retrievers, there will be different levels of desire in the individual pups.

Their personalities, too, will be as different as a nursery full of human babies. Some will resent training and the pressure that a trainer has to apply to make a finished dog. Some dogs will be aggressive, some will be submissive. Others will do all the work, take all the training pressure, and their tails will never stop wagging. Some retrievers need only small doses of correction in training; some need all the trainer can dish out. Cotton likes to see a tough dog, yet one that is intelligent and sensitive to training pressure. But, most of all, he wants to see desire.

"Those are the dogs that keep you going out there day after day," he said.

Cotton pours more Pepsi into his glass and talks of "reading" retrievers and how important it is for a trainer to understand why dogs read differently in certain training situations.

"Shoot, you can look at a dog out there (in the field), after you've worked him awhile, after he gets a little older, and you can damn near read that dog – know what he's going to do before he does it," Cotton said.

But, all the while you're learning to read the dog, the dog is learning to read you. Dogs are especially sensitive to body language. When you hover over the dog, does he cow and grovel? This is a submissive reaction to your dominant posture. With pups or older dogs who are showing the results of too much pressure, get down on their level, kneel down, smile and clap your hands. Watch that tail come up. Watch the bounce go back in their step. You're communicating.

The retriever will throw the trainer curve balls throughout training, and the trainer must react correctly. The trainer must know when to put the pressure on to accomplish the most desirable results.

"Why did he do that?" is one of the most common thoughts a

trainer will have as he works a dog through a training situation. Experience helps the trainer answer those questions. Cotton stresses the importance of knowing the dog. A trainer has to do more than just go through the motions; the effective trainer practices reading his dog during drill work.

Is he running as hard as he did yesterday? if not, why not? Is he consistently running a bowed line on a lining pattern? If so, why? Is the terrain creating the problem? The wind? What exactly makes this dog do what he is doing?

And remember, just because a dog reacts a certain way in a given training situation doesn't mean someone else's dog will react the same way. Every dog, like every person, reacts a little differently to life's little obstacles.

Many of the people Cotton has worked with in his 50 years of experience with retrievers lacked either the energy, the dedication, or the sensitivity to be effective trainers. These are key words for the would-be trainer to remember: energy, dedication, and sensitivity. Cotton adds that flexibility in your thinking also is important.

Just because another trainer has had success with one program or method of training does not mean you will have the same success with another dog. You have to be flexible: If your teaching breaks down, if the dog gets stubborn, you must use a different approach.

Read your dog. Why does your 16-week-old puppy quit bouncing out to pick up the tennis balls you throw for him? Is he bored? Is he tired? Pay attention to him, learn his reactions to different situations. How long before the pup quits playing with the tennis ball?

The trainer, whether he is working with one dog or 20 dogs, needs to learn each individual's personality and training characteristics.

The Program Should Fit the Dog

Cotton will be the first to tell you that there are many good retriever training books on the market today. Each offers a step-by-step guide by which to bring a puppy to the level of a finished retriever.

While Cotton offers a basic training "program," development is based not on rigid training deadlines and a regimented system of training, but rather on the drive, intelligence, and athletic ability of individual retrievers.

Although Cotton deals with individual dogs and their problems, he also has worked with many dogs who had far fewer problems than their owners. Therefore, not only must a trainer evaluate a dog's performance, he also must evaluate his *own* performance as a handler. It is naive to believe that a finished retriever can handle any situation. You will never get 100 percent efficiency, mainly because no one can train a retriever to deal with every situation he will encounter in a day's hunt. Training cannot duplicate the spontaneity of the hunt – not for the dog and not for the trainer.

For the sake of example, let's use a boat full of duck hunters at sunrise:

The young, black Labrador retriever, Pete, sits on the bow of the boat. Motionless. Inside the brushed-up boat, two hunters blow hail calls at the flock of mallards far across the lake. The ducks, fighting the wind, bend slightly. More calling. The ducks see the huge decoy spread and set their wings 200 yards out. But they're cautious, up they go over the boat to circle.

On the third pass, the ducks flare slightly. Something doesn't look right to them. Two of the hunters, noticing the telltale signs of a hasty exit, come out shooting. A single greenhead peels out of the flock and hits the water at the far edge of the decoys. A cripple. He immediately heads for the brush along the far bank. The anxious handler sends Pete, who has been steady throughout.

Pete hits the water and swims through the decoys toward the splash. He puts up a hunt when he reaches the spot where he saw the bird fall, but there's no bird. Pete's handler, now standing on the bow of the boat, blows a "sit" whistle and casts the dog with a left-handed "over."

The dog cuts right. Another whistle, another cast refusal. The duck is working his way deeper into the cover. There is a general confusion going on at the other end of the boat as one hunter gestures, describing the great shot he just made to the hunter who had failed to score.

Pete's handler screams "No!" The dog starts to swim toward him. Another "No!" Pete turns, nose in the air. A frantic "sit" whistle follows, accompanied by a violent left-hand "over" that almost sends the handler/hunter into the icy water. The dog takes the cast only slightly, then scallops back toward the bank. The handler, seething now under his parka, lets the dog land and again tries to handle the dog to the left. Pete finally takes the cast, tail between his legs, up the shoreline. As he crosses the path where the duck hit the bank, his tail starts flagging, he becomes animated again, and into the brush he goes.

A few minutes later Pete reappears with the greenhead in tow.

"Finally," the frantic handler says. "Damn Dog. I know he can handle better than that. I've trained him!"

Typical response. But let's take a look at the situation from the dog's perspective:

Pete watches the sky, watches the birds circle. He is the real hunter, quiet, intense. He senses more than sees the birds' caution. He licks his chops.

At the sound of the shots, Pete leans forward, muscles twitching, ears peaked. From Pete's eye level, the bird appears to fall beyond the wall of decoys. He sees the splash, but is a tough mark because of the poor depth perception provided by his low elevation.

His handler barks his name and Pete dives into the cold water. He swims a straight line through the decoys, as he was taught. But there is no bird beyond. He does what he has always done in training when he sees a bird go down, he begins a controlled hunt.

A strong wind is blowing across the decoys. He hears the "sit" whistle and turns, treading water. Camouflage netting has blown off the side of the boat motor, revealing a bit of white. The duck obviously noticed this, and Pete's eyes are attracted to that end of the boat too. He sees a man waving his arms.

He tries to obey the cast that looks like something a traffic cop might do during rush hour. Another whistle, same result. Then the scary "No!" This is a warning to Pete and when in trouble it's always best to head back toward the handler. He looks closely at the camouflaged boat and finally sees the man on the bow. The handler, wearing camouflage, blends in perfectly against the steep, heavily timbered bank behind the boat. The man is almost invisible to the dog, whose eyes are only inches above the water.

As Pete tries to determine which cast to take, he has to look around and over several decoys. The cast, he finally understands, is directly into the wind. He gives it his best but breaks off, scalloping back to avoid fighting the wind.

Then there is the bank. He has gotten into trouble before for landing where he shouldn't land. But there haven't been any more whistles and "no's." So carefully Pete gets out of the water, tail between his legs.

There's that whistle again.

Finally he picks out the handler from the rest of the movement in the boat.

Pete shudders. The cast will send him along the shoreline and he always has been taught to never run the bank. The bank is not a good place to be. But Pete answers the cast, moving slowly, tail between his legs, down the shoreline.

Bird scent!

This he can handle on his own. And there are no more whistles. He finds the bird and he knows that this always makes the man happy.

So, there is more to effective handling than going through the motions.

Rather than panic when Pete refused the first cast, the handler should have considered why, and the first place to look was inside the boat.

The first thing the handler should have done was tell his buddies to sit down in the boat and shut up. Then he should have taken off his camouflage gloves and shown the dog the spread fingers and palms of his hand as he moved his arms from the elbows in a waving fashion to provide the most visible cast.

Then he should have called the dog back into the water after he landed, hacked him parallel to the bank to the point where the duck landed, and then given him the "hunt 'em up" trill with the whistle. Why go to this trouble? Because this was the way the dog had been trained to make this type of retrieve.

When Pete finally took the cast the handler wanted, then scalloped back because of the wind, the handler should have realized that was going to be the toughest cast to get.

The biggest mistake, though, was probably in the very beginning. The handler could see the duck swimming away. He should have handled from the start to change the dog's mind. This communicates that, "The fall you saw is not where I want you – I want you over here." By the way, handling away from a marked fall involves advanced training and a lot of hard work on the part of both the trainer and the dog.

In a nutshell, the duck hunter in this scenario did not read his retriever. The dog was sending him messages, and the handler, probably more concerned with the escaping duck and his buddies in the blind, was not receiving.

Did the trainer think that just because he was hunting, the dog's training was put on hold? Cotton says that's a bad attitude.

"You've got to concentrate on working a dog when you're hunting with him, the same as you do out shooting with him in a training session," Cotton said. "You've got to accomplish what you start, in other words. You can't let a dog get by with something while he's hunting that he wouldn't get by with in a training session. Say the dog doesn't want to get in the water while you're hunting. Then you've got to make him do it. You've got to go ahead and concentrate on your dog work, the same as you would if you were in training."

The Good Trainer: Objective and Firm

Mentioned earlier was the fact that a retriever trainer has to have energy, dedication, and sensitivity, good qualities to accomplish just about any kind of work. The trainer also must evaluate his or her own personality, especially tolerance levels. Any retriever, regardless of breeding and upbringing, is going to try those tolerance levels. A dog seldom accomplishes a task simply because it is asked of him.

Cotton believes that a good trainer is objective in his attitudes and firm in his corrections. The good trainer uses force and praise at the appropriate times – when they are deserved. Above all, the good trainer must be a patient teacher, and a teacher establishes lesson plans and goals. So before getting into a training session, decide what is to be accomplished. Plan ahead.

Like any kind of learning, retriever training deals with building blocks. You must build on the dog's natural abilities and training fundamentals.

When the dog gets into a training situation that is over his head, which invariably happens, teach by simplifying. For example, if the dog is asked to do a triple mark, that is three birds shot before the dog is sent to retrieve, then teach him the triple by doing every bird first as a single. This reduces the triple to its most simple elements.

Above all, avoid competition during group training sessions. This is not a needless warning. Monitor your own excitement level when every dog at the training session has to be helped on a marking series and your dog waltzes out and hammers every bird. Training sessions are for training, not for winning.

The Good Trainer Reads His Dog

Cotton Pershall has an uncanny ability to read retrievers.

"It's something you've got to learn, though," Cotton said. "I've been at this game for better than 50 years and I've trained thousands of dogs and handlers. The dogs make a lot of mistakes, but the handlers make more."

Therefore, whether it is simple obedience with a six-month-old puppy or a 300-yard water blind with an open all-age field trial dog, try to pick up the signals the dog is sending, Cotton said. How does the dog react to praise? How does he react to pressure? If the dog performs a task perfectly and he gets loved up, then he ignores his next few commands, what can be deduced? Praise may be more than this dog can take. If this is the case, save the praise for the end of the training session. Don't get the dog into bad habits or into a pressure situation because of the urge to pet him. Praise makes some dogs better and some dogs worse.

The flip side of praise is "nagging." Most people will do it subconsciously. "Heel, Duke, heel...come on now, heel. No, no, no... heel, now, come on Duke, heel." Nagging is just putting off the inevitable. Put the lead and choke chain on him. Be firm. *Make* him heel.

"You can't just blindly go through any kind of training program and expect to learn anything about your dog or get him even close to a finished dog," Cotton added. "Books can tell you how to train, how to drill, and all that stuff. But it's awful important that you learn your dog. If you can understand your dog in training sessions, you've got a better chance of picking up the birds in a hunting situation."

Cotton explains that although a trainer needs to develop a basic program for his young dog, seldom will a dog be able to follow the program without encountering problems.

"These aren't machines we're dealing with here," Cotton explains. "They have their bad days and their good days just like people. Sometimes they can't seem to understand no matter how many times you show 'em a particular training test. You just have to struggle through and be patient. And you have to remember that it takes time to bring a retriever along to the point where he can be called a finished dog. This is not something you get done in a few weeks. And even after the dog is trained, he's going to need the experience – the hunting."

Aside from a training program, which Cotton will help develop for the owner-handler in this book, he said that the proper training grounds and training equipment play a big part in developing a young dog.

Good training grounds need a variety of terrain such as rolling hills, ditches, tree lines, field roads, and levees. The cover also needs variety such as pasture grasses, standing crops (which become harvested crops in the fall), mowed cover, tall cover, plum thickets, sedge fields, and so on. There also needs to be a variety of water such as open lakes, stick ponds, potholes, and water-filled ditches.

In most cases, the trainer has to work with the grounds that are close at hand, but keep in mind: If a dog isn't trained on picking up birds that are shot across brush-choked ditches, don't be upset when he doesn't pick up a bird in that situation during a hunt.

The dog must learn to overcome obstacles in a controlled situation – a training situation – before he can be expected to overcome obstacles in the spontaneous circumstances of a hunt.

When looking for training grounds, keep in mind that variety will make your dog a more well-rounded hunter. Check with state fish and game people to find out about public land in a given locale and the dog-training regulations that apply. A word of caution: If the trainer has access to game birds and plans to use them in training, follow state regulations carefully.

In this day of leased hunting rights and pay-by-the-gun hunting privileges, a training lease may be in order if there is a consenting landowner nearby. Quite often retriever clubs buy both training and field trial leases from farm owners.

Next, try to find a retriever club nearby. The best way to locate a club is to check with local pet shops and veterinarians. If that fails, try the fish and game people again. Retriever clubs generally have a few members who are retriever addicts – people who train every spare moment and spend every spare dime on their field trial or hunting dogs. These people will talk retrievers at the drop of a hat and usually train before work in the morning and/or after work in the evening.

The training experience – with the people, the dogs, the guns, and other equipment – prepares the dog for the excitement and near-chaos of the hunt.

The would-be trainer also needs a few basic tools to get started: a

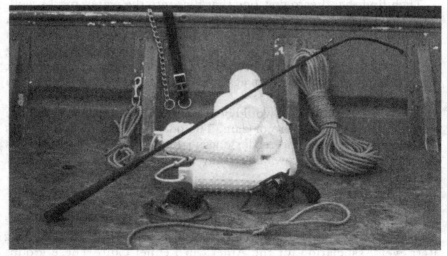

The retriever trainer needs a few basic tools: a nylon collar, a chain collar, a short lead, a lead about 10-feet long, another lead about 50-feet long, a whip or riding crop, a blank pistol and ammo, and a couple of whistles. (Randy Sissel Photo)

dozen white plastic bumpers, a chain collar, and at least three lengths of leads – one about 18-inches long with a loop in the end, one about 10-feet long, and another about 50-feet long (the latter leads should have brass snaps attached). Waterski rope works well, especially in water work where it floats and will not readily tangle in underwater debris. The trainer also will need a stiff riding crop, a blank pistol and ammunition, and a good whistle – preferably two.

Cotton figures that anyone who buys a dog-training book does so for one of two reasons: The person is an organized, methodical individual who is considering buying a hunting dog and training it himself and he bought the book before he bought the dog to give himself an idea of just what will be involved in reaching his goals; or, the person is like the rest of us, which means he already has a dog that is a holy terror in his neighborhood. He drags home shoes, bones, tree limbs, laundry, and dirty diapers. This person mistakenly thought that because he bought one of the retriever breeds, the dog would be a natural hunter and he would never have to go over his waders again chasing cripples through the decoys. This person has begun to realize that someone is going to have to train this meathead before he is going to be of any value at all.

If the trainer falls into the former category, Cotton's advice is look at pedigrees and the work of a lot of retrievers. If goldens are the breed of choice, look at goldens; if Labs tickle the reader's fancy, look at Labs and so on.

Then find that dream dog, one that flies into the water, marks well, has a good attitude about training, and has learned to handle. Cotton suggests, at this point, that the reader look at the pedigree and then go back to his sire and dam for a puppy. Why? Because the breeding has produced at least one good retriever. There is no guarantee that the combination will come up again, but at least the odds on getting a good one have improved.

The second best choice would be to arrange a breeding between the dream dog and a good sire or dam. The odds are not as good on this arrangement because the reader doesn't know what kind of puppies the dream dog will throw. They may be like the dream dog or they may not.

The third best choice, Cotton advises, is looking at paper, at pedigrees. Look for field trial titles such as FC (Field Champion), AFC (Amateur Field Champion), or the hunting titles granted by the Hunting Retriever Club of America, The North American Hunting Retriever Association, or the American Kennel Club. These groups also publish newsletters that list current breedings. You also can find litters of high-quality puppies for sale in the *Retriever Field Trial*

News, published by the National Retriever Club and the National Amateur Retriever Club. Pick out the most attractive litter and get on the waiting list. If you make connections with a retriever club, there will probably be a few members off whom you can bounce pedigree questions.

If you already have a dog, read on and let's hope he is a trainable animal.

"Just because you have an AKC registered Labrador retriever or a golden or something doesn't mean you have a hunting dog," Cotton said. "Every dog is different. Some are athletes and have the brains to make a finished dog. Some don't. It's up to the trainer to make this decision. There is no sense wasting your time with a dog that doesn't like to retrieve. There's too many of 'em out there that do."

In the past few years, there have been a lot of dogs trained at Cotton's kitchen table. A lot of training problems have been solved and a lot of training philosophy shared. But Cotton, the pragmatist, says that retrievers are made more with hard work and perseverance than by any particular method or philosophy shared over cold drinks.

"There aren't any great secrets to training retrievers," Cotton said. "Shoot, I'll tell anybody that asks anything they want to know about training. Anything I've learned in my 50 years at this game. I guess the most important thing, though, about training is that you have to work at it. It ain't easy."

Cotton has trained retrievers when he had to cut paths through the snow with a tractor and a blade. He has trained in the rain and the heat and, yes, even in the cool, pleasant days of fall.

Cotton pushes away from the kitchen table and stands. His whistles, tucked into his shirt pocket, hang from a woven leather lanyard around his neck. They are always there, like a tie on a businessman. He ambles across the kitchen floor and opens the door.

"C'mon, let's get those pups worked before it gets too hot."

Chapter Two

PUPPY TRAINING: FROM INFANTS TO JUVENILES

As we cross the backyard, the pups bounce off the gates of the kennels, yapping excitedly. The older dogs stand wagging their tails, watching us.

Cotton goes to his pickup and comes back with a tennis ball of suspicious origin and a piece of cotton rope with a loop in one end.

He lets out Ruff, a three-month-old Labrador retriever. His little black tail moves back and forth faster than an old woman's fan at a revival meeting. He makes a fast track around the woodpile, then around the duck pen, loops back around the kennel, and is headed for the pond when Cotton calls him.

"Hey Ruff, hey, hey...come in here you little so-and-so." Ruff stops and looks back. Cotton shows him the tennis ball and here he comes. The loop in the rope goes around his neck. Cotton holds him gently with the simple, homemade lead and teases him with the tennis ball.

He pitches it across the gravel drive and Ruff gives chase immediately.

"Oh, he's a goer, now, that one is," Cotton said.

And so the making of a retriever begins.

Puppies: Leads, Tennis Balls, and Loading

Cotton's puppies get started anywhere from seven to 12 weeks with tennis balls. There is something maddening to a pup about the

Cotton uses a tennis ball or a solid rubber ball to get his puppies animated and excited about retrieving. It's all play at this point. Cotton teases the pup with the ball then gives it a pitch. (Michael McIntosh Photo)

way the ball bounces away from him that, plus easy grip and weight, make the balls a natural retrieving object for pups.

Some puppies will return immediately with the ball, some will lay down and chew on it, others will want to take it to the woodpile or back to the kennel for future gnawing.

"At this stage it's a good idea to coax the pup back to you by clapping your hands, whistling, waving another ball or bumper, anything like that," Cotton said. "If he has a place in mind where he wants to go, though, position yourself between the pup and that place. A lot of times it will be the kennel because in the past few weeks, that dog house has become his home. So when you throw the ball, make sure you're between him and the kennel."

Cotton said it's important to get the pup crazy about the ball. Bounce it in front of him, tease him, and then pitch it while he's in a position to see it rolling away. If the pup returns with the ball, pick him up with the ball in his mouth and praise him.

"Let him hold onto that ball and love him up good," Cotton said. "Then do it again. It won't take long before he starts to lose interest. So at the first sign of him getting tired or bored, stop the retrieving. Let him go smell the ducks or something."

At about this same time, Cotton starts putting his little rope leads on the pups.

"The rope gives you a little more control of the pup and breaks him in kind of gently to a collar and a lead," Cotton said. "Instead of

Cotton demonstrates the proper way to handle the pup on the short lead. The hand nearest the dog always goes down in front of the dog before he is sent to retrieve. The off-side hand, in this case the left hand, is used to control the dog. (Michael McIntosh Photo)

grabbing the pup by the scruff of his neck, you can grab the rope. Now you don't want to knot the end because the knot might hang between his toes when he's running and give him some pain. It's a good idea to put the rope on him when he comes out of the kennel and let him run with it on. Eventually, the rope's just another part of the pup's world and he gets used to the neck pressure and it's not such a bad thing. The earlier you can get the pup used to the rope, the better off you're going to be."

Cotton said that at some point, a pup will get it into his head that he needs the ball worse than you do. At this point, after the pup has become accustomed to the short rope lead, you can bring a longer lead and a collar into play. Different lengths will let you stretch the pup out as he gets more proficient in retrieving the tennis ball.

It's important, Cotton said, that you just coax him back with the long lead.

"You don't want to get rough with him, jerking him around," Cotton said. "The only kind of lead pressure he's had so far is the little rope lead, so he's not ready for a heavy hand on the lead. Just

39

kind of guide him, pull him on in, and praise him. Then, let him hold the ball."

What if he drops the ball?

"You're going to have to watch that," Cotton said. "Don't yank him hard enough to cause that (dropping the ball). If he does drop it, get up there and throw it again. Don't get too far back. Keep the lead taut like a fishing line, like you're afraid you're going to lose a trout."

At about the same time the pup is learning about leads and tennis balls, you can start working on loading, Cotton said.

When you put the pup back into his kennel or into his crate aboard your truck or car, simply start telling him to "kennel" or "load." Through repetition, the dog will understand the command. As with so many commands the retriever learns, though, understanding a command and actually performing the task do not necessarily go hand in glove. Nevertheless, Cotton suggests getting him accustomed to the command from the earliest stages of training.

"You have to help him do it at first," Cotton said. "Later on you'll have to *make* him do it."

Puppies: Simple Obedience

So far the pup, from six weeks to about 12-weeks old, is getting used to leads, he is retrieving tennis balls, and he is learning to "kennel."

Now we are going to add a simple obedience command to the class schedule. Like teaching him to kennel, repetition will be the teaching tool.

"All right, now. You've got that short lead on him all the time when he comes out of the kennel," Cotton said. "Hold onto the lead, which means holding his head up, and push his rump down. Not hard or forcefully, but firmly. When it's on the ground, say 'sit.' Then pitch his tennis ball. Let him go right away and when he comes back, go through the same thing again. He gets a retrieve when he sits."

As the pup is returning with the ball, whether he has to be coaxed with the long lead or whether he is returning on his own, start adding the command "heel."

"Heel" will eventually mean that the dog should come to your side. Basically, Cotton teaches two obedience commands – "sit" and "heel." When the dog is told to "sit," he should sit until told to do something else; when he is told to "heel," he should come to Cotton's side and stay at his side. If Cotton walks back to the truck to get a bumper, he might tell the dog to sit, which means that the dog sits until Cotton comes back. He might tell the dog to heel, which means the dog should stay by his side as he walks to the truck.

"This is all play training and repetition in the beginning," Cotton said. "You can't be rough on puppies. It's awfully important that they have a lot of desire to retrieve. When they come out of the kennel, they ought to be busting to go. If you start jerking them around when they're babies, you'll get them all cowed and piggy-acting."

Puppies: Birds, Bumpers, Guns, and Water

Cotton introduces birds to the pup as early as practically possible. Pigeons are generally the bird of choice.

"Birds should always be your ace in the hole," Cotton said. "Birds should get that pup fired up and wild to go. You don't want to use birds too much with pups because they can get to where they don't want to pick up bumpers. But they ought to know about birds. You can take a six or seven-week-old puppy and tease him with a dead pigeon and get him all hopped up and then toss it for him. Try to get several short retrieves out of him that first time and then maybe you wait a week and turn him loose on a clipped-wing pigeon, one that won't fly away but that can walk and flap ahead of the pup. This generally makes them wild about birds.

"Whatever you do, though, don't use a live duck on the pup. If that duck cracks him a good one with a wing or clips the pup's nose with its bill or digs a toenail into the pup, you might wind up with a pup that's afraid of ducks – or he might go in and kill it. Either situation can lead to problems."

If you don't have pigeons conveniently available, freeze the one you killed for the pup. You can use it again in the future.

At this point, the pup is mad about retrieving a tennis ball and loves the taste of feathers. Now, if the pup is physically big enough, start mixing bumpers into the retrieving routine.

"I prefer the plastic bumpers over the canvas or cloth bumpers," Cotton said. "The plastic are cheaper, they last longer, and are easier to clean up. Some of the canvas bumpers will start to rot after awhile and they can mildew and collect dirt and stuff easier than the plastic bumpers. One good time, though, to have canvas bumpers around is when the dog is teething, about four or five months old. The canvas is definitely easier for the dog to hold and when his gums get sore during teething, they're easier for him to retrieve."

Cotton likes to introduce bumpers like this: Throw the tennis ball and let the pup bounce out after it. By this time he ought to be burning rubber to get the ball. Upon his return, take the ball, stick it in a pocket, and whip the bumper around in front of the pup, shake it in front of his nose, try to get him lunging at it, and then toss it a few feet. The first time the pup might run to it, smell it, and then return, looking for the ball. Pick up the bumper, tease him again, and pitch it where he can see it. Tease him and coax him until he decides the bumper is a good thing to retrieve.

If the pup just won't pick up the bumper, but he has shown a definite taste for feathers, tape a pigeon wing to the bumper. Go through the teasing process again and throw the bumper. Be sure the wing is taped securely to the bumper or he will try to tear it off.

When he picks up the wing-wrapped bumper two or three times in succession, go ahead and give him the ball again. Then give him the bumper. Have another bumper, wingless, ready in your hip pocket. After he picks up the tennis ball, throw the winged bumper; upon his return, throw the wingless bumper. By mixing up the retrieving objects like this, you should have the puppy retrieving all of them in short order.

A word of caution: Don't get frustrated with the pup, especially if he shows good retrieving desire for the ball or the bird. With patience and enough gentle coaxing, you should have him picking up all three objects in just a few days.

Most pups, by the time they are 16-weeks old, will be picking up about anything that gets thrown for them, from rocks to shotgun hulls.

When the pup is just mad about bumpers, start "play fetching" him. This will prove especially helpful in future training, when the pup is formally "forced" to retrieve. To play fetch with the pup, simply kneel down and tease the pup with the bumper, holding it firmly. Tease him until he is lunging and snapping at the bumper. Lure him back and forth in front of you and, when he is really animated, let him have the bumper. Play fetch with him several times a week at this stage and gradually introduce the command "fetch" just before you let the pup have the bumper. This simple puppy drill greatly reduces the problems that you may encounter with the forced retrieve when the pup is older.

At about the same time that the pup is learning about bumpers and birds, introduce him to gunfire. This can be done in conjunction with birds if the dog is maniacally inclined to retrieve or it can be done, as practically every retriever trainer suggests, during the pup's daily feeding.

Either way, Cotton says to start maybe 75 yards away from the pup with a .22 blank gun and gradually work toward him. If he likes birds, have an assistant stand about 75 yards away and shoot the blank pistol while the pup is chasing a clipped-wing pigeon. Over a period of a couple of days, decrease the distance until the shooter is standing near the dog while he chases the pigeon. Then move back and start over, using a shotgun instead of the blank pistol.

Cotton teases the pup with a bumper (above), then lets the pup snatch it (below). By "play fetching" the pup and adding the command "fetch" just as the pup takes the bumper, you can probably save yourself time in the forced retrieve phase of training later on. Some pups, strictly due to repetition of this drill, will start fetching the bumper out of your hand on command. (Michael McIntosh Photos)

If you opt for the feeding method, just put the pup's food in his kennel, wait until he is really chowing down, walk about 75 yards away, and shoot the blank gun a few times. Try to work in closer to the dog over a period of three or four days until you're standing beside the kennel door to fire your shots. Then start over using the shotgun.

Cotton said a surefire way to prevent gunshyness or noise shyness is to start when the puppies are just a few days old. While they are nursing, drop the bitch's food pan a few times, clap your hands, and so on. Regardless of how you make the noise, make sure the puppies are nursing when you try this. The association, which is obvious, is with feeding.

Back to birds.

Don't rush the pup on ducks or pheasants. He has plenty of time to learn about these big, tough game birds. Keep him working with pigeons until he shows the aggressiveness and retrieving desire necessary to deal with the toughest bird in the pen. It is important to remember that although the dog must like birds, he also has to like bumpers, because these will make up the bulk of your "training birds." At this point you have to make a few judgment calls about your pup. Is he getting sluggish about retrieving? Is he only mildly interested in retrieving bumpers? Will birds get him fired up again or is he just going through a phase of adolescence?

You will probably have noticed by now that when the pup misses a day or two of play retrieving, he comes out like gangbusters at the next training session. Use this to your advantage. If the pup begins to show complacency about retrieving or seems sluggish going out or returning, no matter how much coaxing he gets, put him up for a day or two. If you just have to get him out, give him obedience work or take him for long walks. One of the best methods, though, to rekindle that retrieving desire is to let him watch a training session from the sidelines.

"Leave him in the crate and let him watch other dogs," Cotton said. "This really builds 'em up. I used to chain a bunch of 'em out like that – choke chains around their necks and hooked onto a cable (staked at both ends). I would stake 'em out like that just where they couldn't get to one another. Then we'd be out here workin' and they could see us. If you got a dog that's layin' back, that will build him up."

Even at this early stage in your dog's training, Cotton says you have to start reading your dog. He will have mood swings, emotional highs and lows, and maybe even a touch of laziness – a major part of training and handling a retriever is reading his reaction to outside stimuli.

Does your pup have a lot of go? If he does and if he really likes bumpers, start him on a few simple *sight blinds*. A sight blind is a training term for retrieves that are made when the dog sees a bird or bumper placed in a certain location – not necessarily a shot bird or a thrown bumper – and doesn't go until commanded. Sight blinds or memory blinds are generally used to build a dog's confidence and to teach him *lines*. A line is the path the dog takes to make a retrieve. In most cases, the trainer teaches the dog to take a straight line to the bird, whether it is a fall that the dog has seen or a true blind retrieve.

"One of the first things I do is teach the puppy to run a line," Cotton said. "I put out a half a dozen dummies and I start the puppy running sight blinds at maybe 35 to 40 yards – bare ground or a mowed field. The bumpers are placed one behind another, in a line, and he can see them."

Cotton starts his puppies on lining drills as soon as they show the necessary retrieving desire. Make sure the pup can see the bumpers and don't worry if he doesn't pick up the bumpers in order. It's more important that the pup goes with enthusiasm. Don't wear him out or bore him with this drill! (Michael McIntosh Photos)

If the pup will sit still for you, let him watch as you put the bumpers out. If not, stake him out while you place the bumpers. If the farthest bumper is at 40 yards, make the closest one about 10 yards. Then hold the pup in a position where he gets a good look at the first bumper in the line and let him go. At the same time, say "back" with enthusiasm. If the pup picks up the first bumper in the line and returns, set him up again and send him for the next one, and so on.

What if the pup doesn't go?

"Walk out there, tease him and throw one" (back down the line to the point you were trying to run from), Cotton said. "Bring him on back and get him kind of keyed up (teasing and coaxing with your voice). Hold that pup back with the short lead or with your hands. It's just like holding a fighter. If you hold a fighter back, he wants to fight even worse. Holding a puppy back gives him a tendency to want to go forward. It usually makes 'em really want to go. Use just a little tension, then let him go!"

After the pup becomes proficient at this game, you can work your line of bumpers back into a loosely scattered pile. Make sure the pup can see the pile. When you progress this far, another minor problem may crop up: The pup may hover over the pile of bumpers, picking up first one then another bumper, as if he can't make up his mind which one to retrieve. Cotton says you will need to fix this.

"Move up to where you're close to the pile and give him a little correction," he said. "There are several ways to do this. Holler 'no' and tell him to heel. Or you can use a check cord on him. Tell him that you know how many are out there. But don't correct him on the second or third dummy he picks up – about the fourth or fifth. Use that 'heel' command."

At this point, then, you are learning to read your dog while he is learning to retrieve balls, birds, and bumpers and perform simple sight blinds. If the weather is right in your part of the country, the pup also needs to learn about water. And, Cotton adds, the pup should be the one to decide if the water is too cold, not the owner. Begin by taking the pup to a lake, preferably with gradually sloping banks which allow for plenty of wading water – wading water for the pup, not for you.

Take the pup for a walk along the shoreline. Does he get his feet wet and then jump out of the water? Does he run and splash in the shallow water? What does he tell you about the water? If you read his reaction as "the water is too cold," then come back later in the season and try again. But if he shows no trepidation about getting wet, try tossing a bumper into the wading water. If you get a retrieve, keep throwing, nice and short. If you don't get a retrieve, keep coaxing and teasing and keep your tosses close to the bank.

If the pup shows no reluctance about retrieving from the wading water, gradually make your throws longer. Take it slowly. If you can get the pup in up to his belly the first time, settle for that and come back again later in the week.

Start again with a walk up the shoreline. Has the pup's attitude about the water changed? Give him a few short retrieves, stretching him out to the belly-deep water. Then try one a little longer, just far enough that he has to swim a few strokes.

At this point, you'll probably get the "tip-toe stretch," where the pup goes as far as he can and still touch bottom and then tries reaching for the bumper. Coax him, splash a few stones near the bumper. If the pup just can't get up the nerve, you might have to take your shoes and socks off and get in with him, coaxing and cajoling until you get him swimming.

There is an alternative to getting wet – an older dog, one that gets in the water unhesitatingly. Tease both dogs with the bumper, give it a pitch, and let them compete. You may not have to throw a bumper to get the pup in the water and swimming. The older dog, playing in the swimming-depth water just beyond the shore, may provide enough incentive for the pup to try his water wings. Keep in mind that all the pup's experiences up to this point have been positive. Keep it up in the water; make the water a good place to be.

All of the training described so far is basically play training, with emphasis on the word *play*! And while all of the skills described are important training steps, the most critical thing a puppy can learn about in these first few months is people. As a trainer, you must have the dog's best interests at heart. Take the pup with you as often as you can. Establish a bond, a friendship with the pup. The more serious training that the pup will endure as an adult will be easier for both of you to deal with if you like each other.

Juveniles: The Trainer as Disciplinarian

The puppy is maturing. He is about six months old now. You have made him a retrieving fool. He is picking up everything you throw for him. He is using his nose well, and he is returning as aggressively as he is going out.

He is doing short sight blinds and the puppy lining drills. You can tease him with a bumper and he jumps and lunges at it. His simple obedience training has been done with little pressure, relying largely on repetition to get your message across. You have been using your homemade rope lead and he is so accustomed to it he barely notices it's around his neck.

He is still sometimes dropping the bumper when he gets near you, and he tires of retrieving after six or seven throws. Some days he wanders on his return, distracted by smells and sparrows. Some days he is a superstar; some days he seems to forget what his assigned role in life really is. But he is happy nearly all the time and he would rather be in the car or truck with you than about anywhere else he can think of.

You endured the teething phase with him when he was about four or five months old, but his teeth are solid now, his gums are no longer bleeding. It's time that he started learning what a real working retriever does for a living.

So go back to the basics: obedience training. The pup understands the commands "sit" and "heel." Sit means, "Sit 'til I tell you to do something else," and heel means, "No matter where you are or what you are doing, get in here by my side and stay by my side."

Of course, until now, the pup has had no pressure to respond to these commands. But, if he is to become a worthwhile companion in the duck blind or on the pheasant hunt, he has to learn that your commands are the most important things in his life.

"They have got to have a solid foundation of obedience," Cotton said. "I think, really, if he is a high-strung dog, he needs it at least once or twice a week throughout his life. I mean, let him know that when you say 'heel,' it means '*heel!*'

"Start off with a chain (collar) and a lead – a five-foot lead. And then start him on obedience, very strict obedience. Heel! Sit! Walk him around, making him sit and stay and then I would have him come to me on command. I would use his name and the word 'heel' and blow the whistle, toot! toot!"

Proper Obedience Requires Drill Work

Up until now, training for you and the pup has been like recess. Now it becomes work, for both of you. The chain collar and the five-foot lead replace the homemade lead, and the honest-to-goodness training begins.

The first step is to put the chain collar on correctly. Cotton prefers the large-linked collar that fits loosely around the dog's neck. The collar should be large enough that there is no pressure on the dog's neck when the "active" end of the collar has no tension, the end attached to the lead. It should rest across the top of the dog's neck. The active end passes through the static end of the collar.

For the sake of example, let's say that you have taught your pup to heel on the left side. He also sits on command, but generally, at the slightest diversion, he is gone. This is no longer allowed.

You, as the trainer, have to develop an attitude at the beginning of this formal training that play is play and training is training. Your commands must be given with authority, not loudly, but crisply. There can be no doubt in the dog's mind about which command you have given him.

So you have slipped the chain collar around the dog's head, just behind the ears. He is bounding around at the end of the five-foot lead ready to play. You command "heel" and tug firmly on the lead – one quick flick of the wrist. The pup, if he is a sensitive one, looks slightly startled and comes into heel. You command "sit" and once more tug firmly on the lead, this time jerking straight up. The dog sits. What is his tail doing? Is it sweeping the ground behind him or is it still? The tail will give you an idea of his attitude to this new pressure.

Now you command "heel" and start walking. If the dog surges ahead, snap the lead and repeat the command, "heel." If the dog lags, again snap the lead and command, "heel." Then repeat.

The chain collar should not be used to drag the dog to you or to reel him in. The chain collar should be used with sharp snaps, jolts, of pressure. Steady pressure on the pup may cause panic.

"Well, you got that five-foot lead, and you walk around and you sit him down, after you have got him heeling, sitting, and coming to you (on the "heel" command), you ought to have him jumping just like a

Training on obedience commands: how you gain and maintain control of the dog. In the drill work on the obedience commands "…you ought to have him jumping just like a frog," Cotton said. Walk the dog at heel, then make him sit. Take off again for a few steps with the pup at heel, then make him sit. Repetition and consistency in your commands are fundamental to developing a responsive retriever. (Michael McIntosh Photo)

49

frog," Cotton said. "When you say heel, he should jump, when you say sit, he should put that butt down immediately. Make him jump like a frog: heel, sit, heel, sit. You've got him thinking then," Cotton said, "His mind is not wandering. When you're training on obedience, you can't let a puppy wander all over. He's got to keep his mind on you. If he wanders, well, he's not going to learn. Now you've got that five-foot lead in your hand and you tell him to sit and then you walk away from him. And if he starts to move, then take the end you're holding and snap it so the (active) end of the chain collar pops him under the chin. Either that or take him right back and sit him down while snapping upward on that lead. And then you walk around in front of him and he is supposed to be sitting there all the time. Then you go back and pet him real good."

Remember, "sit" means "sit until I tell you to do something else." This does not come overnight. But the better your job was with obedience during the pup's play training phase, the more consistent and persistent you were with your commands, the quicker the pup will respond to the increased pressure at this stage.

Cotton recommends several formal obedience drills:

In-Line Heel/Sit Drill – This is his most basic obedience drill. Simply heel the dog in a straight line for about 20 yards, make a 180° turn, and heel the dog in the other direction. Make your turn *into* the dog. This will be the easiest turn for you to make and will require the least correction with the lead. It will be important to use your left leg (with a left-side heeling dog) to guide him through the turn. In this drill, it is important to keep the dog's head and shoulders near your knee. Do not let him surge ahead or lag behind. Remember, use sharp tugs on the lead to work the dog into position, not constant pressure. When the dog has had enough repetition and correction on this drill, he will probably start to anticipate your turn at the end of the line, so change the distance; one time go 15 yards, another time go 25 yards. When this anticipation starts to occur, add the sit command to the drill. Walk the dog down the line and try to get two or three sits before you turn. Then repeat. As a trainer, you must be on your toes. Your corrections with the chain collar should be immediate, whether for "heel" or for "sit."

Cotton also recommends introducing the "whistle sit" after the pup has this drill down solid. Just continue the drill as you have been, except when you vocally command the dog to sit, add a single toot on the whistle. Do this every time you give the command. Eventually you will be able to drop the vocal command and just use the whistle. When the dog shows he understands the single whistle blast, demand the same response to the whistle that you get from the vocal command.

The In-Line Heel/Sit Drill: a basic drill aimed at honing the dog's skills on two obedience commands. Cotton suggests heeling the dog on lead in a straight line for about 20 yards, making a 180-degree turn with the dog on the inside of the turn, and then repeating the procedure. In the beginning, the turns into the dog will require the least correction. (Michael McIntosh Photos)

Later, when the dog has become proficient at the drill and understands the chain collar corrections, you will want to turn away from the dog at the end of the line. (Michael McIntosh Photos)

Inside/Outside Box Drill – When the pup becomes proficient at the above drill, add "boxes" to it. Heel the dog down the line about five yards, command "sit," turn to the left and walk another line for about five yards, command "sit," turn to your left, and repeat until you have reached the point of origin. Make the dog sit at each corner. Exaggerate your directional changes. When the dog has the left turns down, go the other way, so the left-heeling dog has to heel to the outside on the turns. Again, the dog will begin to anticipate the corners and will eventually sit without the command. So heel him through the corners, sometimes. Keep him thinking.

Figure 8 Drill – This drill should come after the dog is doing the inside/outside box drill proficiently. Simply heel the dog in a figure 8, which will put him one the outside on one turn and on the inside on the opposite side of the eight. Use your knee to guide him and keep him from leaning against you when the turn is toward the dog. Use the choke chain and the lead to keep him in the proper position on the outside turn. Avoid the eventual anticipation by varying the size of your turns.

The Clock Drill – This drill should be started after the pup has mastered the other obedience drills and, although it appears simple for the pup to learn, it is an important drill for the pup to master and will help both of you later in setting up an initial line on blind retrieves. Begin with the (left-heeling) dog sitting at heel, both of you facing 12 o'clock. Command "heel" and turn to face 3 o'clock. As you command heel, add pressure to the chain collar. The dog should be sensitive enough by this time to respond quickly, probably too quickly, thinking that you will walk off in that direction. Just use the lead and collar to guide him into the right spot and command "sit." Now repeat, stepping toward 6 o'clock. Then repeat, stepping toward 9 o'clock, and finally back to 12. Now go the other way, counterclockwise, stepping into the dog. This will require the opposite directional pressure with the lead. Help the dog through this. At this point in his training, though, he will probably catch on quickly.

Although many retriever trainers add the riding crop or heeling stick to their training program at this point, Cotton advises against it.

"I don't think you need it yet," Cotton said. "I think that switching cows a puppy a lot. A little praise and that choke chain and lead are all you really need."

Cotton said that your obedience sessions should be short and snappy, maybe 10 minutes. Praise the pup for his good work, but do so with a trainer's eye. What are the results of the praise? Understand your dog. How much praise is too much? Is a simple "good boy" enough, or do you have to really love him up?

The Clock Drill: This drill teaches the dog to follow the motion of the handler's body. By learning to move with the handler in this drill, the dog will be easier to line up for blind retrieves and multiple marked retrieves. The dog should start out facing 3 o'clock. The handler then should step toward 12 o'clock, and coax the dog into the correct position. Repeat the move toward 9 o'clock, and finish at 6 o'clock. Then reverse directions and repeat. (Michael McIntosh Photos)

Cotton also offers a few tips for those of you who own one of those hardcases, a tough dog who barely feels the pressure of the chain collar and who lunges ahead regardless of the pressure you apply.

"You do some reverse marches on him," Cotton said. "In other words, you reverse your direction as soon as he lunges. You say, "heel" and snatch him with that lead and chain. Do more figure eights, too."

Try to determine the dog's weaknesses in his obedience training. Is he slow to turn on the outside of the figure 8? If so, increase the lead pressure as you make the turn. Is he reluctant to get going again after he has been corrected with upward pressure on his neck? If so, use fewer "sit" commands and more "heel" commands.

One more Cottonism for the hunter: Throw a half-dozen decoys on the ground where you will be doing your obedience training and leave them there. If the pup shows interest in them, you have the chain collar and the lead on him and you're working on obedience commands, so say "heel" and give him a sharp tug on the lead. By the end of your formal obedience training, he should be ignoring the decoys.

Now, add these advanced obedience drills to your list:

The Extended Sit Drill – Start with the 50-foot lead on the pup and gradually work out to the end. Make the pup sit as you walk away, first to about 10 feet. Turn and face the dog. While holding the lead and repeating the "sit" command, walk in a clockwise circle around him. Now walk the other way. Nail him down with that "sit" command when necessary. The pup probably will want to keep his eye on you as you walk the circle. Let him turn to watch you, but don't let his tail get off the ground. The pup, at some point in this drill, will break. When he does, react quickly. Command "sit" and use the technique Cotton suggested earlier – whip the lead so that the chain collar pops his chin. If this does not get his attention, take the pup immediately back to the spot where he was sitting, command "sit," jerk upward on the lead (as you have been doing on the other obedience drills), make him sit, and repeat the drill. Your goal is to work out to the end of the 50-foot lead. When the dog is good at this drill, you will be able to command "sit" and tug gently on the lead and the dog will not break. As a matter of fact, he will probably staunch up at the pressure. It is most important to be alert in this drill and to be persistent. The pup must do it correctly, but take it in steps; don't expect perfection on the first day.

The Heel/Here Drill – The pup must be doing the Extended Sit Drill before you can move on to the Heel/Here Drill. For this drill, you will need the 10-foot lead, the 50-foot lead, and your chain collar.

The Extended Sit Drill: The retriever must learn that he sits on command and maintains that position until instructed otherwise. Cotton starts this drill with the dog on a long lead. He commands "sit" and steps away from the dog. Then he moves in a circle around the dog to test his obedience. (Michael McIntosh Photos)

The Heel/Here Drill: Cotton makes the pup sit, walks to the end of the lead, and commands "heel" or "here." The lead gives the handler control of the situation. This also is a good drill to work in the whistle command for "here," usually three or four quick blasts of the whistle. Use the lead to guide the dog into the proper finish at your side. (Michael McIntosh Photos)

Sit the pup, step to the end of the 10-foot lead, turn and face him, and command "heel" followed by three quick toots of the whistle. If the pup has been thoroughly trained on the Extended Sit Drill, he may be reluctant to respond. If so, drop the lead, kneel down, clap your hands, and coax him to you. As the dog comes in, use the lead to guide him into position. Ultimately, he should come directly to the proper side, his head at your knee and his body curling around to the outside until he is in the heeling position. *Do not let the dog circle you to come into heel!* If you do, that circle will almost immediately start growing in size. Keep the dog in sight and under control. Start close on this drill. Repeat until the dog is doing the drill perfectly on the short lead and then start stretching him out. Remember to use the whistle command in conjunction with the vocal command. He must obey both commands without hesitation. It is most important, especially in the early going, to praise the dog for obeying the command.

The goal of all obedience training for retrievers is control, but it must be done in degrees. You know you are making progress when the dog is doing the drill work with slack in the lead.

"You got to keep his attention on you," Cotton emphasizes. "A finished dog should never tug on that lead. He should walk loose on that lead. And if you tell him to sit, that's where he should be. If you let him scout around and cheat, then he'll expect to get by with it when you do your other training."

Obedience drills create the foundation for everything your retriever must learn, but don't go overboard. If you do nothing but obedience drills whenever the pup comes out of the kennel, before long he'll probably climb into the dog house when he sees you coming, so mix up your training sessions. Work on marking right along with your obedience drills.

Marking for Juveniles

From the age of about seven weeks, the pup has seen you throw objects for him to retrieve. Hopefully, by the time the pup is three or four months old, he is picking up your handler-thrown bumpers and returning with them in good shape.

At this point, though, Cotton suggests enlisting a friend to help throw *marks* for the pup. Marks, as you can imagine, are birds or bumpers that the dog sees fall, thus "marking" a spot.

Cotton says to start the pup on marks thrown by gunners in the field as early as is practical. Start close, with the assistant simply attracting the pup's attention with a shout and a shot from a blank pistol, and then tossing the bumper. It is best to start these types of marks on a mown field where the pup can go immediately to the bumper without hunting for it.

Do not worry about making the dog steady at this point, that is, holding him back or making him sit until you release him. Simply line him up where he can see your assistant in the field, and hold him

Marks for the beginner: Start relatively close to your bumper thrower, Cotton explains. Call for the throw, and if the pup has paid attention to the fall, send him on his name. If he is successful, move back 10 yards and repeat. (Michael McIntosh Photos)

with the short lead looped around his neck. When you think the pup is looking at the assistant, raise your right hand to signal for the throw. As soon as the pup tenses as if he wants to go, release the lead and say his name – "Ruff!" If the pup is successful, move another 10 yards away from your assistant and repeat. Depending on the enthusiasm of the pup, four or five of these marks will probably be plenty, especially if you move farther away from the "fall" after each retrieve.

This type of marking drill does several things for your pup, Cotton said. First, it makes him look afield, where he needs to be looking, watching for birds; second, it enables him to run through that handler-thrown barrier, that static distance determined by how far you can throw a bumper; third, it enables you to start conditioning your pup; and fourth, it teaches him a line to the mark.

Think about it: You are moving the pup in a straight line farther away from the fall every time he retrieves. Basically, you are teaching him a long mark by breaking the line down into short, simple retrieves. You will be surprised at how fast you will be able to move back to 60 or 70 yards for these puppy retrieves. If you have a real "goer," you might be able to get 100-yard retrieves out of him in just a couple of days.

Distance, though, is not as important as proper technique at this point, Cotton said. So keep the marks simple and make sure the pup can see the bumper fall. If you're not sure, get down on your knees and have your assistant throw a practice dummy. How does it look from down there?

There are problems you may face when you introduce the pup to the assistant-thrown marks, Cotton said. For example, if he goes to the fall and picks up the bumper, he may take the bumper to the assistant. This is pretty typical for a pup; after all, the assistant (probably someone the pup is familiar with anyway) is closer and the pup, being well-socialized, may think this is the thing to do. Just keep blowing your whistle and calling him to you with the "heel" command. The assistant should just ignore the pup.

The next thing that generally happens is the pup spits the bumper out on the return. Don't get nervous, just take the pup out to the bumper, tease him and pitch it a short distance, and then work back to your initial starting point. You will make the pup hold the bumper when he gets a little older.

Another problem you might face is "hunting short." This generally occurs because of the aforementioned handler-thrown barrier. The pup is accustomed to running only so far and finding a bumper. Now he is going to have to run farther.

This is the way it looks: You have worked the pup back to about 60 yards or so from the assistant. You call for the mark, then release the pup. At about 40 yards, the handler-thrown barrier, he begins to slow down. When you read this in your dog, signal for the assistant to shout and throw another bumper. It is important that the assistant pay attention to what is happening with both you and the dog. He needs to make sure that the dog is looking toward him when he throws the next bumper.

After you do this a few times, the pup should start driving past the handler-thrown barrier all the way to the area of the fall. Again, keep the bumper in mown grass so when the pup does drive to the area, he will quickly find a bumper. Try to cease this kind of help by the assistant as soon as possible. Otherwise, the pup begins to look for another bumper from the assistant rather than hunt for the bumper that is down. Cotton recommends keeping the puppy marks on the mown field until the dog is showing confidence and proficiency, both going and coming.

When you do start throwing bumpers into short cover, decrease the length of the marks. The pup often develops other problems when you make this transition. For example, because you have been making the bumpers easy for him to find, he may hunt in the cover for just a moment and then leave the area or even start to come back.

It is best, especially in the beginning and especially if the pup appears to be a weak marker, to "salt" the mark, Cotton said. In other words, scatter a half-dozen bumpers in the area where the assistant is going to throw the mark. The pup should find a bumper quickly. Over the next few training sessions, you reduce the number of bumpers until finally the pup has to hunt up the single bumper thrown by the assistant.

Cotton advocates repeating any mark with which the pup has trouble. For instance, if you start the pup out with a 40-yard mark on the mown field and work back to 60 yards and the pup starts to hunt short and the assistant has to help him with another bumper, repeat the mark from the same spot. This is one of Cotton's basic training tenets: *If you run into a snag, regardless of what you started out to accomplish, work on the problem and get it ironed out before you move on.*

Water marks should be kept simple at this point in the pup's life. Start him at the water's edge and keep away from marks that are thrown in such a way that the pup can avoid getting in the water to pick up the bumper. The assistant should keep a pocketful of rocks handy so he can guide the pup to the bird or bumper when he runs into trouble. Three or four water marks will probably be plenty for the pup. Have the assistant move around the bank so the marks aren't always landing in the same spot.

You may run into a "no go" on these simple water marks if, for example, the pup has picked up three water marks and he's tired and the water is a little chilly. But of course, being the typical, eager trainer, you want to keep working, so you call for one more mark. You release the rope lead just as you did the previous three times, but this time the pup, sitting at your side, just turns his head and looks down the shoreline. This is when you should have a bumper handy. Simply tease the pup and get him fired up and throw a short mark for him to retrieve in the water, then put him up. You will *make* him go later on, but he is too young for that kind of pressure right now.

Cotton suggests training four or five times a week. The work should be split up about evenly – half the sessions on marking, half on formal obedience. As a rule of thumb, Cotton said, you should plan to spend from a month to six weeks on formal obedience training.

Cotton takes the short lead off Ruff and gives him the "hi on" command, a release command that means, "Go on, go play, go leave your signature on a few trees." Ruff heads for the pond. In a few minutes he's back, dripping wet, waiting at his kennel gate. Cotton lets him in and steps over to Jay's kennel.

"Now we really get to work," he said. "I've got to do some force training on this one."

Chapter Three

THE FORCED RETRIEVE: THE PUP GROWS UP

The young yellow Lab, Jay, stands with his paws against the kennel door, tail wagging.

"Hey, hey, Jaybird," Cotton teases the dog, "get down off that gate."

Jay stands back and Cotton opens the kennel gate, bringing the dog quickly to heel. We walk down the field road past the kennels where there are no distractions. Cotton tells the brawny pup to "hi on" and while he's piddling, Cotton ruminates about force breaking.

"On young dogs, very, very seldom will you ever get one that just rolls all the way in on water retrieves," he said. "He'll generally drop that bird and shake if it's kind of cold anyway. Then he'll readjust and get hold of it and come on in. You'll have to do a lot of coaxin' on 'em to make 'em come on in.

"Sometimes they'll spit out a crippled bird and the damn bird will run off. That's why you'd like to have 'em force broke. But they have to know what 'fetch' and 'hold' is before you get onto them too rough while they're out there working."

For a few minutes, Cotton stands there, arms folded across his chest, watching the yellow pup romp.

"Jay, heel!" he shouts.

The dog comes into heel and Cotton snaps a lead onto his collar. The force training session begins.

Teaching "Hold" and "Drop"

The force retrieve has a variety of names: the conditioned retrieve, force fetching, force breaking, and so on. Conceptually, the forced retrieve involves a conditioned response in the dog. In this case, the conditioning will be achieved by pinching the retriever's ear flap. The response, if conditioned properly, will be an instantaneous "fetching" of a bumper or bird.

As a rule of thumb, most retrievers are ready for the forced retrieve when they have been through their formal obedience training, somewhere between seven and nine-months old, although the forced retrieve can be taught to a dog at any age. At about seven months, though, the pup will start sending you signals that he needs this type of conditioning.

"A good signal is when the dog starts getting sloppy and doesn't want to bring and hold the bumpers," Cotton said. "Then you're going to have to start force breaking him. There's never a dog that doesn't get sloppy sometime. You're going to have to put the bumper in his mouth sometime in his life, and you are going to have an awful session. You can't get away from it. They are animals, they just don't do it right all the time."

Once the dog masters the forced retrieve, the trainer has a most effective training tool. As a matter of fact, the forced retrieve and obedience training may be the most important training a gun dog can have. During this force breaking, you will learn about your dog's personality and his intelligence. You also will learn about his training sensitivity.

When you start working on the forced retrieve, stop all training on marks. At this point, all your energy and that of the dog will be aimed at this one phase of training. Marking and the resultant sloppiness in the dog's return, that is dribbling the bumper, spitting it out at your feet, and so on, detract from effective force breaking.

"Don't associate retrieving with your force breakin'," Cotton said. "Do the force breakin' on the side. Remember – you got to have the dog know what 'fetch' and 'hold' is before you get on 'em out there when they're working."

If the dog has responded well to your formal obedience training, you will have an easier time with force breaking. This training can be done in a backyard, a garage or basement, or any other area free of distractions. You will need a nylon or leather collar, the 10-foot lead,

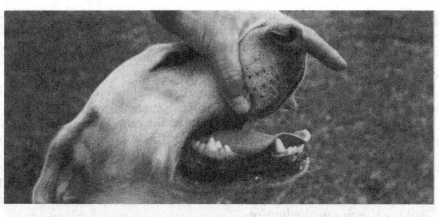

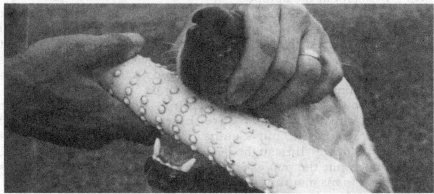

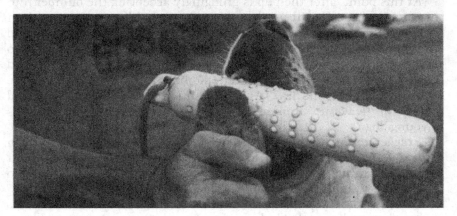

The "forced retrieve" begins by teaching the dog to "hold" a bumper. Make the dog sit. Force his mouth open by placing the palm of your left hand across his nose and pinching inward with your thumb and middle finger. After you have forced the dog's mouth open, insert the bumper and immediately hold his mouth closed by grabbing the skin under his chin and lifting upward. (Randy Sissel Photos)

a plastic bumper, and a canvas bumper.

Begin by putting the collar around the pup's neck and attaching the lead. This will give you a convenient handle with which to move the dog around. Tell the dog to sit. Be firm with your sit command – no slips.

Kneel down and force the pup's mouth open by placing the palm of your left hand across his nose and pinching inward with your thumb and middle finger. This pressure will force the pup's lips in against his teeth as well as giving you leverage. Insert the bumper into his mouth with your right hand and immediately grab the skin under his jaw and hold the dog's head up.

You will probably have to grab the pup's collar with your left hand to help control his head swinging. In most cases, the pup immediately will try to spit out the bumper.

If you fail to successfully juggle dog, bumper, and collar and he spits the bumper out, simply say "no" and try again. You will eventually get it. At the same time, do not let the pup break your sit command. Since the pup is not sure yet just what in the world you're trying to do, don't introduce the command "hold" until the pup is actually holding the bumper for a few seconds.

While you're doing all this juggling, keep another thing in mind: the pup's lips. Make sure, by running your thumb and forefinger around the pup's gums, that he does not have either an upper or lower lip caught between the bumper and his teeth. You do not want the pup experiencing any discomfort when he has the bumper in his mouth.

At this point, after the pup is grudgingly accepting the bumper into his mouth, he will still not be consistent in holding it. Remind him firmly to "hold" by putting your forefinger under his lower jaw and pushing upward in the V-shaped slot just behind his chin. You also can tap the jaw upward with your fingertips, repeating the command "hold." Eventually, the pup will sit and hold the bumper without the pressure beneath his jaw. At this point, introduce the command "drop" or "leave it." Remember, you are teaching. Be gentle; this is a young dog.

Exaggerate the hold command when you begin teaching "drop." In other words, make the dog hold for 15 seconds or more after your original command "hold." This span of silence between the two commands will help the dog differentiate.

Now, gently reach for the bumper and command "drop." At this point, the pup has probably been dropping the bumper as soon as you reach for it anyway. This is a passive way to introduce the command. Eventually, though, when it is clear that the dog understands the drop command, you will want the dog to hold even after you grab the bumper, not releasing until you command "drop." Later on, this will prevent you from having to chase a duck around in the boat when your dog, anxious to go get those other two birds down in the decoys, releases the bird before you have a firm grip. Likewise, this is another element of control, and control is your goal.

When you reach the point where you feel the dog knows the command, reach for the bumper and if he drops it, simply command "hold" and reinforce the command by putting the bumper back in his mouth and tapping him under the jaw. Then reach for the bumper again, and just rest your fingers on it, commanding "hold." When the

Test the dog on the "hold" command. While he is sitting at heel, put the bumper in his mouth and then walk him through an abbreviated heeling drill
(Michael McIntosh Photo)

dog continues to hold with your hand resting on the bumper, then let him release it when you give the command "drop."

Now, what if the pup doesn't drop the bumper when you reach for it? First, try holding the bumper, commanding "drop," and blowing in his nose. In most cases, especially in the beginning, this will make the pup release the bumper. If not, open his mouth with your left hand in the manner that you started the hold drill. Later on in the force breaking, you may have to pinch the dog's lip against a canine tooth to get the drop.

When you are satisfied that the pup understands the two commands and he is holding until you tell him to drop, test him, Cotton said. Put the bumper in his mouth, command "hold," then go through one of the heeling drills with the pup. If he doesn't hold when you command him to heel, and he probably won't, simply stop, put the bumper back in his mouth, reinforce with a light tap under his chin, and continue the heel drill. Every time he drops the bumper, just command him to "hold" and put the bumper back in his mouth.

You will get a variety of responses. As soon as you say "heel" and begin to step forward, some dogs will spit the bumper out, tail wagging, and take off with you. Some dogs, tail between their legs, will gently put the bumper down and come to heel. Some dogs will come to heel and drop the bumper after they have walked a few yards or when you make the first direction change. Then there are those who will bounce up, tail wagging, come into heel, and hold the bumper through the entire drill.

Regardless of the attitude, be gentle and take your time. The dog must understand that "hold" applies even when another command comes into play. With enough encouragement and reinforcement, the pup will heel with you, hold the bumper, and be happy about it.

When this step is accomplished, it is time to move on.

Introducing the Ear Pinch

The pup is holding and dropping proficiently now, so it is time to add the conditioning, the ear pinch, and the command "fetch" to the force breaking sessions.

Many trainers have created elaborate methods to get through this type of training. Cotton said that he has used a variety these methods depending on the dog, but the simplest way, requiring the least amount of preparation and equipment, is to use the nylon or leather collar and your five-foot lead.

Begin as you started the hold training. Kneel down next to the dog and command "sit." Again, be firm with the command. If the dog

Introduce the ear pinch from the same position you started teaching the "hold" command. When the dog opens his mouth in protest to the pressure on his ear, insert the bumper, release the ear, and command "hold." (Randy Sissel Photo)

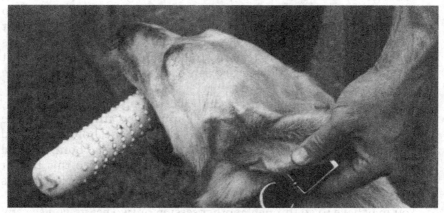

Some dogs may require more pressure on the ear that you can get with just your thumbnail. If that's the case, pinch the dog's ear against the edge of the buckle of his collar. (Randy Sissel Photo)

heels on your left, reach behind his head and hold the left ear flap in your left hand, between the thumb and edge of the forefinger. Hold the plastic bumper in front of the dog's nose, dig your thumb into the ear flap, and when the pup opens his mouth in protest, slip the bumper into his mouth, release the pressure on the ear, and tell him to "hold."

Keep the pressure on the ear until the pup gets the bumper into his mouth, Cotton said. You want the dog to understand that the only way to get the pressure off his ear – the only way to make the sting go away – is to get the bumper between his teeth.

In the early going, get the bumper into his mouth as quickly as you can, Cotton said, and don't use any more pressure with the ear than is absolutely necessary. Cotton said there will be a wide variety of reactions to the pressure on the ear. A sensitive dog will react vocally and immediately. At the other end of the spectrum is the hardcase. You won't even get a reaction out of him with the thumbnail against the forefinger. He'll probably just sit there and wag his tail. For these, Cotton has used a small bolt through the dog's collar. Put your left hand under the collar and fold the ear flap over the bolt and apply pressure with the thumb against the bolt. An "in-between" dog may require laying the ear flap over the buckle on the collar and merely applying pressure with the meaty part of the thumb.

Why reach across the head and pinch the offside ear? Because if the dog's reaction is aggressive, to bite, he will turn away from you and toward the ear that is being pinched. This is a reaction that occurs more often in older dogs than in seven-month-old pups.

Throughout the force training, talk to the dog in calm, reassuring tones, Cotton said. Avoid making the dog panicky. Strive for the pup to accept the pressure as just another part of training. Try to conduct a force training session once a day and get it over with as quickly as possible. You might be able to force train some dogs twice a day. But if the dog starts to get depresssed, go back to one session per day. Remember, read your dog.

Now, let's say the first pinch, between thumbnail and forefinger, went as planned. Let the dog hold the bumper and stroke him on the chest. Tell him what a good dog he is. Repeat the hold command while you stroke him. Then command "drop." Take the bumper, hold it in front of the dog's nose, and pinch the ear again. Do this five or six times in the first session. Notice that the command "fetch" has not been used.

You may have to go through another session or two before you see any progress. But at some point in those first few sessions, as soon as you put the bumper in front of the dog's nose and pinch the ear, he is going to reach out and take the bumper on his own. This is just what you want.

Now introduce the command "fetch," followed by the ear pinch, and put the bumper into the dog's mouth. When the pup will take the bumper on the command without the pinch, move the bumper an inch or two below the dog's nose and farther in front. Command "fetch"; if the dog does not reach immediately, pinch the ear and he will go for the bumper. When the dog will get the bumper at this new, lower level without the ear pinch, take it down another couple of inches.

Move the bumper downward in one or two-inch increments until you finally get to the ground. You may have to spend a week or more

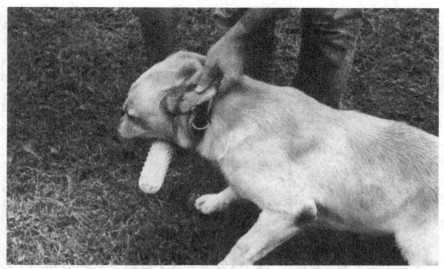

When the dog is responding to the pressure on the ear by grabbing the bumper that is right in front of his nose, start gradually moving the bumper closer to the ground. If the dog balks, put pressure on the ear and make him grab the bumper. (Randy Sissel Photo)

getting the bumper to the ground. Don't rush. Be thorough. You will probably notice that just because the pup fetches at a new level once doesn't mean he will do it again without a pinch. Try to get four or five fetches without a pinch before moving on to a new level.

Once you get the bumper to the ground, the hard part begins. Get your four or five fetches without a pinch while you're holding the bumper on the ground. This means holding one end of the bumper off the ground a couple of inches and the other end of the bumper resting on the ground. Now, set the bumper on the ground and rest your fingertips against it. Command "fetch." Be ready to pinch immediately and guide him down to the bumper. Remember, keep the pinch on until he gets the bumper in his mouth.

When you get three or four fetches without a pinch, start moving your hand away just as the dog's mouth gets to the bumper. Be ready to add the pinch – because when you move your hand away, the dog may balk.

Once the dog picks the bumper up as you move your hand away, you are getting somewhere. Move your hand away earlier and earlier until you can place the bumper on the ground, move your hand away, command "fetch," and the dog will pick up the bumper. Have that ear flap ready to pinch at all times.

You are going to make mistakes during this process. Most of the time the mistakes will involve indecision – not pinching when you

Once the dog is fetching the bumper consistently, put one end of the bumper on the ground, hold the other end a few inches higher, give the command "fetch," and be ready to add the pinch. When the dog is successful at this level without the pinch, lay the bumper on the ground and just rest your fingers on it. Give the command "fetch" and be ready to add the pinch. (Randy Sissel Photo)

need to pinch. That's okay; it will just take you a little longer to get the bumper to the ground. You also may run into another problem at this point: The dog will take the bumper off the ground and just keep his head there, his chin about an inch off the grass. That's okay, just tell him to hold and tug upward with the lead. If he drops the bumper, command "fetch" and pinch him again.

At this point, you are still kneeling beside the pup, your hand on the collar or the ear, and he is fetching the bumper off the ground with confidence. Now take your hand off the ear. If the pup fetches correctly, place the bumper on the ground in front of the pup, stand up, and command "fetch." If he balks, simply reach down for the ear, command "fetch," and pinch.

When you are standing up and getting four or five clean fetches, move the bumper a foot out in front of the dog and start to build momentum. Take a short step toward the bumper and command "fetch." If the dog balks, pinch the ear and move him into the bumper. Try to get him moving from the sit position to take the bumper. This means that you must move too. Speed the retrieves up here, develop movement and momentum. Add a little excitement to your voice, but don't let the dog have the bumper until you give the command.

Test out the "fetch" command when the pup has fetched four or five times in a row off the ground without a pinch. Don't intimidate the dog by holding the collar or the ear. Just place the bumper on the ground in front of the pup and give him the command. (Randy Sissel Photo)

At some point, you will have to start holding him back because he has become so thoroughly conditioned that he will want to get the bumper in his mouth even before you give the command. Remember, you are the one in control, not the dog. If he tries to get the bumper, enforce the "sit" command and tug upward on the lead.

During the course of force training, the dog probably has gotten a bit depressed. Now is the time to start bringing him up. Praise him, good-dog him, and work the bumper farther and farther away. When the pup is moving with confidence to pick up the bumper at a distance of four or five yards, you are there. Throw him a few play bumpers – get that tail flagging again.

When do you call the job complete?

"He's force broke when he will fetch on command off the ground,"

Cotton said. "Game – ducks or pheasants. Then I think you have gone far enough."

If you do not have access to these game birds, use the canvas bumper and check out the "fetch." You'll find that you might have to use a pinch to get the dog going on the new object. But it shouldn't take much work to get him picking up the canvas bumper just like he was picking up the plastic bumper.

The forced retrieve training is over at this point. You could have spent from a week to six weeks on this work. All dogs are different – a few will go through it quickly, a few will take forever, at least it will seem that way. And just because the dog has been forced to retrieve, don't think his mouth problems are over, Cotton said. The dog may still have a sloppy mouth, especially with bumpers. At least now, though, you have a few training tools with which to correct the problem.

For instance, when the dog comes out of the water with a bumper or a bird, command "hold." He knows the command – make it stick. If he drops the bird or bumper anyway, tell him to "fetch." If he doesn't, use your tool, the ear pinch. Gradually, his return will improve.

Cotton advises caution when using the ear pinch with young dogs in the field.

"Don't go out there in the field when he drops a dummy and jump down on his neck. Do it gently. Otherwise he'll think, 'If I go out there, I'm going to get punished.' When I was doing that real forcing (formal training), I sometimes would come back a little later (after the formal session) and even let him chase one and grab it. Then I'd say, 'That's a good dog!' Force break him gently."

Even after the force training, some dogs still have a lot of puppy left in them. This type of dog often will pick up his bumper or bird, flip it around, and dribble it on the ground, playing with it. What do you do?

"He's been force broke," Cotton said. "And he knows what 'fetch' is and he knows what 'hold' is. Pinch that ear and say, 'Now fetch it and hold it.'"

Your marking work upon coming out of force training should be relatively short, simple marks. This gives you more control and allows the dog to be immediately successful. Keep the pressure off. Some dogs, especially sensitive dogs, may need to have a few birds shot for them to get them going again. Use your new training tool sparingly; keep the pup's attitude upbeat.

One other problem will crop up. You may have seen it in the puppy even before the formal, forced retrieve training began – snapping at the bird or bumper as you were taking it from the dog's mouth. This needs to be stopped immediately. If not, you may find yourself playing tug-of-war with your dog over a nice, fat greenhead.

"Say, 'no!' and eliminate all that play fetching. You've played with him to fetch it and he's got that in his mind," Cotton said. "So you eliminate that right now. Don't associate that with his work any more. Now, when he starts doin' that, pop him (with a crop). Eliminate that in association with his work."

Cotton warns against starting your marking training again before the dog is thoroughly force trained. He tells of a pup he acquired that had stopped retrieving because her former owner had hurried through the forced retrieve training.

"She associated that with going out there to retrieve and she didn't think she should," Cotton said. "Then when she went out there and didn't want to pick up the bumper, she'd just drop it. She was afraid she was going to get punished. I just built her up. And when she wouldn't pick that bumper up, I just easy-done it. I used the play method and a little correction (ear pinch) with it. Hell, I had her where she was really wantin' it in just a couple of weeks."

Cotton adds that if the dog responds aggressively, as if he might bite, during the initial stages of the forced retrieve training, consult a professional trainer. But don't expect miracles – the pro may not be able to work with the dog either. And if the pro says, "Get rid of the dog," get rid of the dog. There is something inherently wrong with a pup that bites the hand that feeds him.

"Old D.L. (Walters – a professional retriever trainer in LaCygne, Kansas) had some experience (with biters)," Cotton said, shaking his head. "He had his stomach laid open a couple of times. Yes he has. He was tellin' me once that a dog hooked into him and I said, 'What did you do, D.L.?' and he said, 'I said nice dog...leave it...come on now...leave it.'"

Cotton chuckled, and added, "That's when you have to tie the dog down (to a wall). You've got him tied up there and he has got to do what you want him to do. And he can't come to you."

Cotton finished Jay up and we walked back up the field road toward the kennel. Jay, not particularly bothered by his force breaking session, sprinted for the lake where only a few minutes before Ruff had taken a swim. We met him at the kennel.

Smoky, a black Lab about 14-months old, looked through the wire next to Jay. Smoky stood at the kennel gate, tongue dripping, his dark eyes were fixed on Cotton. Cotton opened the gate and Smoky leaped out of the kennel and in two bounds was in the back of Cotton's pickup.

"Looks like he's ready to go," Cotton said. "Let's head down to Saline and throw some marks."

Chapter Four

LAND RETRIEVES: MARKS AND BLINDS

We stopped at the house and picked up Cotton's "grandbabies" as he so proudly calls them. Mandy, a willowy little blonde, and her younger brother D.J. – about 60 pounds of curiosity and mischievousness – rode in the back of the truck down to the Saline Valley Wildlife Area.

The wildlife area is tucked between two high ridges just a few miles northeast of Lake of the Ozarks in central Missouri. For the retriever trainer, it offers a spring-fed marsh full of watercress and tules surrounded by wooded hillsides, pastures, and fields planted to crops.

Cotton turned right off the pavement onto a gravel road and crossed a low-water bridge. A narrow strip of bottomland opened up to the left. Cotton stopped the truck, hopped out, and fumbled around in the pickup bed, eventually uncovering three orange bumpers. He walked across the field of overgrown wheat stubble and dropped the bumpers near a utility pole in the middle of the field. Cotton returned and we drove another 200 yards down the gravel road before he pulled off. Everyone piled out of the truck.

"D.J.," Cotton said, "Cut Smoky loose."

Smoky rolled out of the crate, looking for Cotton.

"Hi on, Smoky, Hi on," Cotton said. He fumbled in the back of the pickup once more and finally came up with a "heeling stick" and his short rope lead. Smoky, having taken care of his bush business, literally bounced alongside Cotton with enough nervous energy to light the nearby town of Eldon.

"Heel," Cotton commanded. He slipped the lead around Smoky's neck and they walked across the field to a worn spot in the grass. Cotton looked across the field to where he had dropped the orange bumpers, 200 yards away. He stepped forward with his right foot. Smoky, heeling on the right, crouched, tail stiff behind him, muscles quivering. Like a radar-equipped missile, he was locked on.

Cotton put his hand down in front of Smoky's head, palm toward his leg.

"Dead bird, now, dead bird...*back!*"

Smoky slung sod up behind him as he rocketed toward the spot where Cotton had dropped the bumpers. He drove on a straight line across 80 yards of broomsedge, down through a tree-lined ditch, and across the wheatfield to the bumper pile. He returned the same way. It was obvious that Smoky had done this "blind" retrieve before. Cotton took the bumper and sent Smoky back to his crate.

"All right now, Mandy, you and D.J. take about six bumpers apiece and go out across that field there and I'll tell you where to go. Now pay attention when you get out there and don't make Grandpa mad."

The grandbabies, like little soldiers, marched into the field. Cotton, hands folded across his chest, watched the children's progress. He shouted instructions, then had each child throw a practice bumper. Both children were, as you might expect, amazingly adept.

"All right," Cotton said. "What we have here is a double. One mark (thrown bumper) thrown to the right from the right-hand gun and another thrown to the left from the left-hand gun. The right-hand gun is across that little depression and the left-hand gun is closer, on this side of the depression. See the concept? He picks up one on this side and one on the other side. We'll shoot 'em one (motioning to the right-hand gun) and two (pointing to the left)."

He uncrated Smoky and brought him at heel to the "line," the spot from which Cotton would work. Smoky's head swung first to one gunner and then to the other.

"D. J., you first," Cotton shouted. Then he waved his left hand. D. J. shouted, "Hey, hey," and threw his bumper. Cotton put his hand down, as he did before on the blind retrieve, and sent the dog: "Smoky...*back!*"

Smoky, in his characteristic fashion, fairly flew out to the spot where the bumper fell, looped through the spot twice, picked the bumper up, and returned. Then Cotton did Mandy's mark, shorter and to the left. Smoky had a longer hunt, but he stayed in the area where he had seen the bumper fall and eventually picked it up.

"Now, we do the double," Cotton said. He signaled first for D. J. Smoky, tongue dripping, stared intently. Then Cotton called for Mandy's bumper. At her shout, Smoky turned away from the longer bumper and watched the second bumper fall. Cotton, right foot out, put his hand down and sent the dog. Smoky banged the first bumper and on his return, he squared up perfectly for D. J.'s mark. Cotton put his hand down and sent him.

Smoky was a black streak on his way for the second mark. He returned in similar fashion, deep chest heaving only slightly. At heel, he turned to the left of the two marks, looking toward the utility pole near where the orange bumpers lay.

"Dead bird, now, dead bird," Cotton said. The hand went down and Smoky, in anticipation, left just as Cotton uttered the command. His line out and back, again, was perfectly straight.

"Good dog, Smoky," Cotton said with a grin. "Now, hi on, go on, now, hi on." And such are the basic skills that a retriever should exhibit in his land work.

Land Marks: Four Component Parts

Land marks are, of course, birds or bumpers that the dog sees fall, such as you might run into on a dove hunt or a pheasant hunt. The dog must "mark" the fall, then go to the area and hunt until he finds the birds or bumper.

This looks pretty simple on the printed page; it's a lot more difficult out there where the birds are flying. A good marking dog needs sharp eyes, an ability to locate the guns on report (usually derived from experience), perseverance, and a good nose.

At this point in training, your pup should be thrilled to death about retrieving. Mostly he has had handler-thrown marks and, whenever you have had the opportunity, marks thrown by gunners in the field. From this point on, you will need help teaching marking – wives, sons, daughters, neighbors, or anyone else who has a little idle time. Eventually, people will start running into their houses and slamming doors when they see you and your dog coming down the street. At some point, though, maybe through a retriever club, maybe through a hunting acquaintance, or maybe just by blind chance, you will find a person or two who will become as addicted as you are. Treat these people with great respect, remember them at Christmas, and verbally admire their skill.

Before you start putting gunners in the field, though, Cotton recommends developing a basic marking philosophy and establishing training goals. This works, and it helps focus your thoughts while you're standing in the middle of a cow pasture scratching your head watching your dog merrily run over the hill, chasing meadowlarks. Begin by analyzing the "marked retrieve."

First, the dog must be steady so he can mark the falls in cases where more than one bird is shot. If he starts running as soon as he hears a shot, the chances are better than average that he will not see or mark even one fall clearly, especially if you're blocking a draw in a Nebraska cornfield and your fellow hunters are 100 yards away.

Second, the dog must run in a straight line to the area of the fall. Why a straight line? Consider your own marking skills. Let's say you're dove hunting and you shoot a bird that sails across a fence and lands in standing beans 60 yards away. You walk in a straight line to the fence, but before you cross, you notice an open gate about 30 yards to the right. Instead of climbing the fence, you go down the fence to the gate and walk through. About halfway back to where you originally stood at the fence, it dawns on you that the obvious patch of grass you were using to mark the dove's fall was just one of many patches of similar grass. Now which one was it...? Sound familiar? Your chances of finding the bird would have been better if you had kept your eye on the fall, walked straight to the fence, and climbed over.

The same marking philosophy applies to your retriever. It's probably even more important to the retriever because he doesn't have your height advantage. Marking is a lot tougher when you're doing it from knee level, so you will want your dog to run as straight a line as possible to the fall.

Third, after he gets to the area where the bird fell, he has to stay there. He can't just make a couple of passes through the fall and decide he needs to hunt a spot where he found a bird 15 minutes earlier. He has to be persistent, he has to use his nose and hunt intelligently. The latter is derived from experience, especially when it comes to retrieving birds. So the more birds you use in training, the better the dog will handle hunting situations.

Fourth, the dog must return with the bird, delivering it gently to hand. Four steps. You must concentrate on each step during every training session, every time your dog is sent for a mark.

The first problem you will have is "breaking," that is, as soon as the dog sees the bird or bumper in the air, he will surge against the rope lead. This is a good response – he wants to run. You should hold the rope lead in your right hand if the dog heels on the left. As the dog is bucking against the lead, put your left hand down and give your release command.

In most cases, this will simply be the dog's name. Field trial

Use the short lead to start steadying the dog when training on marks. If he heels on the right, like Smoky, hold the lead in your left hand and put the right hand down before releasing him on his name. (Michael McIntosh Photo)

handlers often use the word "back." It is important, though, that you hold the dog for just a moment before you give the command. In every marking session from this point on, hold the dog increasingly longer before giving the release command.

When the dog begins to associate going with his name, make him sit before he gets the release command. For example, when the dog starts to surge against the lead, repeat the command "sit," then make him sit with upward pressure on the lead, the same correction you taught him in obedience training. When the pup sits, still holding the lead in your right hand, put your left hand down and give him the release command. From this point on, the pup never gets to retrieve unless the hand goes down and he is given the vocal release command.

At some point in the early going, the dog may become confused. He has seen a bumper go down, he wants to retrieve, but you told him to sit. Because your obedience training was well done, the pup sits until you tell him to do something else. The only problem will be that the pup may not associate going on a retrieve with the hand going down and his name being spoken. So you have to encourage him, teach him: Walk closer to the bumper, tell him to sit, and have the thrower pitch another one. Then, immediately put your hand down and release the dog with his name.

And remember, deep down in your bag of tricks is the forced retrieve. If after correcting him for breaking he will not go, even after you have tried all the encouraging maneuvers you can think of, you might have to fall back on the command "fetch." Use it to get the pup going only if your encouragement fails. Generally, Cotton said, this is a method that would only be used on older, advanced dogs. Hopefully, any problems will be of the "breaking" nature, though, and not the "no go."

Eventually you will want to hunt the dog without the rope lead. One way to make this transition is to use a nylon or leather collar on the dog with your rope lead slipped beneath it. Get the dog used to the sit command followed by a tug upward on the collar. Then you can begin slipping the rope lead from beneath the collar before you send him.

"He still might even think that lead's on him," Cotton said. "Pick him up with that jerk like that and he'll still think he's got a string in that loop (on the collar). But as far as correcting him and stuff like that, you're going to have to entice him a lot to break and correct him for breaking."

When the dog does break, try to prevent the retrieve if possible. If you can't get the dog stopped, have your bumper thrower pick up his bumper.

"If he is successful," Cotton said, "(that is) goes ahead and gets the bird, do it over on him and then you've got a good opportunity to really get to him."

Cotton means, then, that you "false line" the dog. Upon the dog's return, after breaking, set him up for the mark again and call for the bumper. Put your hand down and wait, get the dog keyed to go, then say a number or maybe all you will have to do is move your hand slightly. One of these things will probably result in a break, at which point you jerk him back with the rope and reinforce the sit command. With a hardcase, you might use a slightly longer rope so the jerk is compounded by the dog's increased momentum.

"Then don't ever let him make a retrieve there," Cotton said. "Move back or go to another spot or something if you are going to let him have one. But don't let him have one of them that you've punished him on. When you're correcting a dog on a problem there like that, I mean a tough one like that, where you've had to almost break his neck, don't give him a bird there. Instead, walk out and throw some dummies or a dead bird but don't let him pick them up. Just stand out there and shoot and throw dead ones here, there, and all around, you know, call a lot of numbers if you want to. You've already punished him for breaking and he's supposed to sit there, right?"

Cotton has a recommendation for those dogs who grow wise to the neck pressure.

"You could have a cord around his waist with a slip knot," he said. "Some dogs aren't going to break with something around their necks, I mean if they think anything is attached to them there. The dog won't even know this is attached to him, hardly, just layin' over his back."

The goal is to make the dog steady when he is hunting. In most cases, you will not be hunting the dog with leads or collars on him. Collars hang in fences and undergrowth and can be extremely dangerous when the dog is working in flooded timber. So the dog has to be steady, even without the collar and lead.

Cotton said putting the hand down before the dog gets the release command is an added deterrent to breaking.

"Put that hand down," he said, "and move it a time or two (as in the false lining correction mentioned above). Then tap him on the nose, tell him 'No! No!' Make him wait for the command."

It probably dawns on you at this point, that the marking training has gone by the wayside. That's kind of the way dog training goes: You set out to work on one thing and another problem crops up. When this happens, break your training session down and work on the problem.

Cotton offers further advice to help steady a young dog.

"Sit him there, make him sit," Cotton said, "and throw a lot of birds, dead birds, or even clipped-wing birds. Make him sit. Walk all the way around him. Then don't let him have one right there because you don't want him to go."

If you're going to give him a bird, go to another part of the training grounds, he added.

As a professional trainer, Cotton demanded "steadiness," even going so far as working a group of 10 dogs at once.

"I'd set maybe eight, nine, ten dogs in a group and make them sit there and I'd call one at a time. I'd work him, put him back, call another, put him back. That kept them steady and also made them eager to retrieve, too (by watching other dogs work). You don't start putting them there until you got 'em broke, where you can set them in a group and call one's name and then another one's name and make them stop. You have them all sit there and I could call one and stop him, then line them up just like soldiers."

But even at that level of training, don't bet your paycheck on the dog's steadiness. You can train the dog his whole life and, generally, if

75-yard "single"

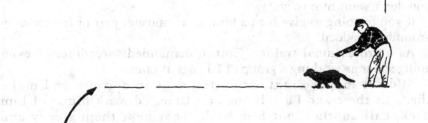

40-yard "single"

"Singles" marking for the beginner. Two gunners or bumper throwers stand at a right angle to the "line," the place from which the handler will send the dog. One gunner stands at about 40 yards, the other about 75 yards. The terrain should be relatively flat, the cover short. Pick up the 40-yard single first, then the 75-yard single. (Art by Christopher Smith) the dog is birdy enough to be an honest-working retriever, he's going to break now and then. All you can do then is try to prevent a retrieve, Cotton said.

While steadiness is an important facet of good marking skills, the trainer also must set up training situations that make the dog concentrate and use his eyes. Marks should be thrown by different throwers (which represent hunters) at different depths – one long, two short, maybe one at medium depth. You get the idea. The dog has to understand that the birds don't always fall at one depth. He must use his eyes, concentrate, judge distance, and remember the falls.

So we begin simply, with two bumper throwers standing in a flat, mown field. Bring your pup up with the short rope lead looped around his neck. Remember, don't tie a knot in the end of the rope that will hang between the dog's toes. Establish a line, a point of origin, from which to run. The dog should run from this spot on both marks.

If you draw lines from your dog to each gun, they would make a "V". The angle between the two sides of the V should be about 90°. Let's say the left-hand mark is 40 yards away, the right-hand mark 75 yards. Do the left-hand mark as a single. Bring your dog to the line, point him at the left-hand gun, tell him to sit, and signal your bumper thrower to throw. The bumper thrower should then throw the bumper angling slightly back. This is done with the hope of teaching the dog to drive past the gunner standing in the field. But, by no means should the gunner throw angling-back throws every time. After the dog starts driving well, then change your throws. Sometimes throw straight out from the gun, sometimes back. Make the dog concentrate on the mark.

So how did he do on the first mark? If he had to hunt at all, repeat it. This is an easy mark, short and with relatively no cover. Try to get a perfect retrieve before you move on. If you have to repeat the mark to get a good retrieve, do it. Then line him up for the second, longer mark. This second bumper thrower should be alert and ready to help the dog at your signal.

It is important that the gunners are at a 90° angle to you. Any closer together and you may have problems getting the pup to look at or hunt the longer mark. After all, he just picked up two bumpers at the first station, why should he hunt anywhere else?

This is where your hard work on obedience comes into play. Remember the Clock Drill? Use it. Swing the dog to the next gun. If he persists in looking at the shorter mark, signal the second bumper thrower to shout. If the pup swings to look in the direction of the shout, have the gunner throw the bumper. Then use the same steps as before on your release. If he still won't look at the second gunner, take a few steps in that direction, walking as close as necessary to complete the second mark.

There are several possible outcomes on this second, longer mark:

1. The pup may hunt for just a moment, look at the closer gun, and decide to hunt there again. If this happens, have the second bumper thrower shout at the dog until he gets his attention. Then have him throw another bumper where the first one fell. This should incite the dog to come back to the correct fall.

2. The dog may start to hunt short, especially if he's had nothing but handler-thrown marks in the past. If this is the case, have the thrower shout and throw another bumper. Use the same procedure you used in Chapter One to make the pup drive to the fall. On the repeat, have the thrower throw one bumper after another while the pup is running to the fall. This should get the pup driving to the area.

3. The dog may hunt deep of the mark. This is okay – he has shown a lot of drive. Let him hunt so long as he stays relatively near the area of the bumper. Repeat the mark.

4. He pins the mark. In this case, don't repeat.

Your goal for this training session should have been to get both marks, as singles, in good shape. Secondary goals would be to work on steadying the dog and to work on the dog's finish, that is coming to heel while holding the bumper.

In subsequent training sessions, use the mown field from a different location. If the field has a little contour, use it to give the dog slightly more challenging marks. Keep the wind in mind; when practicing or training on marks, keep the wind at your back so the dog has to drive deep of the fall to wind the bumper. A breeze in your face might make the dog hunt short or at least drop his nose and start hunting before he gets to the area of the fall. One of the goals you need to accomplish with this type of training is to get the dog using his eyes and marking an area – he shouldn't start his hunt until he gets to that area.

At this point, your pup should be hammering everything you throw at him on the mown field. He's going out with style, stopping right at the bumper, and returning in good shape. You've had up to three gunners in the field throwing singles for you, all at different depths. So let's begin working on "multiple marks," that is, marks that the dog has to remember.

Multiple Marks

A good place to start is that first training situation, with the guns at a 90° angle from the starting point. Bring your pup to the line, tell him to sit, then do both marks as singles. If he completes the two singles successfully, put them together. Tell him to sit and call for the right-hand bird. With all the singles training you have done in the past few weeks, he is getting pretty steady, but keep the check cord in your hand. Let the dog look at the mark for a moment, then call for the left-hand mark. Make the dog wait, put your hand down, call a couple of numbers to test his steadiness, then give him the release command.

When he returns with the first bird, bring him into heel so he is facing the second mark. Grab the short cord, take the bumper from him, and let him look toward the second bumper. When he is concentrating on it, when you think he's got it located, put your hand down and send him. When he returns with the bumper, you've successfully completed your first "double."

There are a number of problems that may crop up to prevent this success. Probably the most common, aside from the obvious break, would be forgetting the first bird down. In other words, the pup picks up the last bumper that was thrown, just like he's been doing with singles for weeks. But when you send him for the second bird – the first bird that was thrown – he either doesn't go or he goes about 10 feet and stops and looks around in a state of confusion. If this happens, simply set him up and do the mark again as a single. Then repeat the double. If he still doesn't get the idea, call him back, have the gunner simply shout to get his attention, and send him again without having another bumper thrown. The gunner's shouts will probably jog his memory enough that he will go. If necessary, walk the dog closer to the fall and coax him into going for the second bird. Through sheer repetition, he should start going for the second bird.

Another problem you may find on the second bird is that the dog starts to go, changes his mind, and veers back toward the area from which he has just come. This is called going back into an "old fall," a common problem, especially when two birds or bumpers fall fairly close together or on nearly the same line.

If this should happen, simply signal the gunner on the right to shout at the dog, get his attention, and pitch a bumper at the one that is already down. Come back and try the double again.

"The only reason they want to go back is that the birds are too close, too tight," Cotton said. "I've never run into that occasion too much."

Cotton said a third problem he has seen involves the young dog quickly giving up his hunt on the second bird of a double and coming back to him.

"I've had a lot of dogs want to hunt and leave a fall and come in to me, but after you have that dog stoppin' and taking a 'back,' then they stop that."

This correction, however, will be saved for later in the dog's training, after he is handling.

Yet a fourth problem that may arise involves the pup picking up the last bumper that was down and racing toward the other bumper that was down. If he manages to get to the second bumper and spits out the bumper in his mouth, this is called a "switch" – not desirable. Try to get him stopped before he gets to the other bumper. Use your obedience commands; call him to heel. You may have to run between the two falls and cut him off – do your best to prevent him from switching. Spread the guns to an even greater angle and repeat the double. Regardless of what happens, try to pick up the double successfully before you conclude the session.

You have been doing singles in different locations with at least two gunners in the field for several weeks, so now start repeating those singles as doubles. Then you can move your singles training gradually into cover. Now you're getting some place.

Your marking fields should have lines of trees and ditches and short cover and tall cover and corn stubble – you get the idea – areas fit for hunting. So you change up. One day you do multiple marks in the mown field, the next day you do singles in the field with cover, and so on. Give the dog diversity. Eventually you will want to do doubles in the hunting field. But wait until the dog is going on the second bird of his doubles (the "memory" bird) like gangbusters in the mown field. At this point, start adding a third bird to your multiple marks on the mown field.

"I do a lot of triples on our dogs," Cotton said. "Long as they'll sit there beside me, I'll start giving them triples." He adds that these are not long marks, and that they are all wide open with no cover.

For the sake of example, let's go back to our original set of singles on the mown field, which became our original double, which we are now going to turn into a triple.

Your two guns, again, are set up at least 90° apart. Take them both first as singles. You should be successful now without having to repeat either single. Now set the dog up and call for the right-hand bumper. Handle the two marks like you would any double, except after the second bird goes down, pull a bumper from your hip pocket and throw it to the far right side. Hold the dog back, then put your hand down and send him for the handler-thrown bumper first. When he comes back to heel, already have yourself aligned for the left-hand bird. When he locks up, send him. Then do the same for the remaining bird.

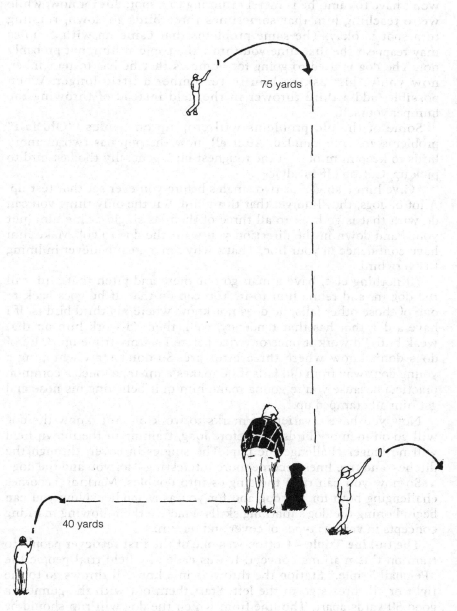

75 yards

40 yards

A "beginner's triple." The same marks that were introduced as singles for the beginner becomes a "triple" when the handler adds a mark from the line. Be sure the dog is handling the singles well before advancing to the triple. (Art by Christopher Smith)

You will probably get this triple the first time you try it because the dog has repeated the other two marks so often, he won't have to hunt; he is merely running to a spot. But for now, while we're teaching him that sometimes three birds go down, running to a spot is okay. The same problems that came up with doubles may reappear the first time you throw the triple at him, but probably not. The dog is used to going for bumpers that he has to remember, now you're just asking him to remember a little longer. When possible, add a third thrower in the field instead of throwing the bumper yourself.

Some of the old problems will crop up on triples. "Old fall" problems are compounded. After all, now the pup has two memory birds to keep in mind. On the toughest bird, generally the last bird to pick up, Cotton offers advice:

"Give him a single, or two singles before you ever set that test up. A lot of dogs, they'll forget that third bird. But the only thing you can do with that is go back to all three of them as singles. Line him (put your hand down in the direction you want the dog to go). Make him have confidence in your line. That's why I'm a great believer in lining to every bird.

"If nothing else, have a man go out there and pitch that bird, call the dog in, and reline him to it. You can do that. If he goes back to one of those other falls, he does not know where his third bird is. If I have a dog that has that tendency, well, then I'd work him on that weak bird. I'd work it once or twice before I set my triple up. A lot of dogs don't know where three birds are. So don't start whipping a young dog away from old falls if he makes a mistake (once a common practice) because you're gonna make him quit believing his nose and get him all cramped up."

Now you have a variety of marks to work on. You know the dog will go on memory birds and before long, training in the mown field will no longer challenge the pup. The singles in cover, through the ditches, and tree lines become more interesting – for you and the dog.

So now you can turn the singles into doubles. Marking becomes challenging both for the dog and for you as a handler. Now you can begin honing the dog's marking skills. Practice the following marking concepts in various types of cover and terrain:

The In-Line Triple – Cotton was one of the first retriever people to train on this marking concept. It was called by field trial people the "Pershall Triple." Station the throwers in a line. All throws go to the right or all throws go to the left. Start them out with the gunners a good 50 yards apart. The line from which the dog will run should be square to the middle gun station. Start close, maybe 50 yards away, and begin this drill as singles. This is a difficult concept for the dog,

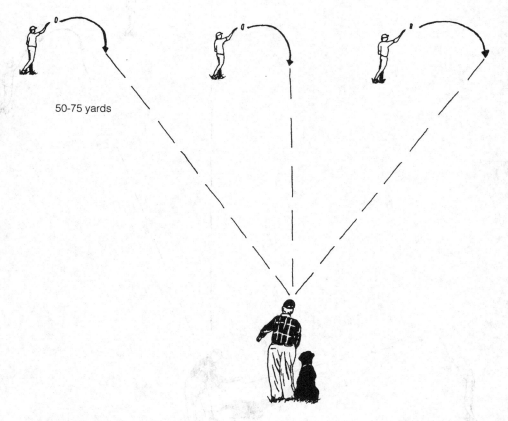

50-75 yards

The "In-Line Triple" drill. As usual, start this drill as single marks. When the dog is doing the singles well, do the middle and left-hand gun as a double, then the middle and right hand gun as a double. Eventually work into the triple. The middle bird will create problems. Be patient; you probably won't get this down in one or two sessions. But when the dog learns this drill, his marking abilities will be well advanced. (Art by Christopher Smith)

The "Indented Triple." After you pick up the left-hand gun, the dog has to choose which mark he will pick up next. If he chooses the right-hand gun, he may drive through and hunt behind the middle gun. The dog has to "check up" on the right-hand gun, that is slow down and hunt before he drives through. This is advanced work. (Art by Christopher Smith)

so take your time and get the singles down perfectly. Then start trying to get the multiple marks. You can train on the middle and left-hand gun as a double and then the middle and right-hand gun as a double. You'll notice how difficult it is to get the middle mark. Eventually step up to doing the triple.

The Indented Triple – Another field trial-born marking drill and an equally tough concept. The two, tight right-hand marks are made especially tough if the wind is blowing from right to left. The dog really has to pay attention to these two birds and be persistent in his hunt. Work the right-hand mark as a single by itself first. You may try to get the middle and right-hand mark as a double before adding the third bird.

The Flower Pot Double – This drill really teaches depth perception to the pup. The two gunners are almost in line. It is important to practice this one as singles – the short one first, then the long mark. Now repeat as a double, same order. The next time you set this drill up, reverse it – do the long mark first, then the short mark. It should be tougher. In most cases, the dog, having been long once, may not want to check up on the short mark. Done as a double, it really becomes tough – but a good drill to make the dog concentrate on his falls.

Cotton advises adding one more marking concept to your training regimen, a training situation that may save you a crippled bird some day – the "switch bird."

This is a situation that happens quite often when the dove shooting is hot and heavy. For example, you knock down a high, overhead shot that drifts out to about 60 yards, falling in heavy cover. You send the dog. He has a long hunt but finally picks up the bird and is headed in. Suddenly, a low flyer appears right in front of you. You shoot and knock it down, and it falls right in front of the dog. What does he do? Does he switch birds? If he does, and if the bird he was carrying is crippled, you might lose it. So prepare for this set of circumstances in your training sessions.

The dog must learn that he doesn't switch birds. He must finish the first retrieve before he is sent for the next bird. So, in your training, as the dog is returning with the last bird of a double or a triple, shout and throw a bumper from the line in a direction that puts you between the dog and the bumper. Remember, you're just introducing this in training, so make it easy on the dog and teach him the desired result. As you throw the bird, tell the dog to heel and, if he ignores you and spits out his bumper and heads for the fresh throw, cut him off. Grab the short lead he's wearing and take him back to the bumper he left, make him fetch, and then call him to you.

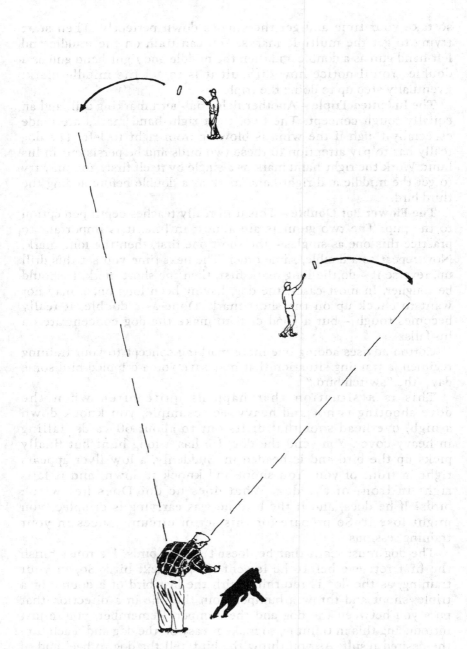

The "Flower Pot Double." This is a good drill to work on the dog's depth perception marking. You also can use this drill to teach the dog to "check up" for a short mark after driving deep for a long mark. Vary the order of the marks from one training session to the next. (Art by Christopher Smith)

When he gets to heel, then you can send for the "switch" bird.

"Then you can move it (the switch bird) until you have it thrown right at him," Cotton said. "You say 'no!' then 'toot, toot' on that whistle. 'Heel!' and just keep on."

Blind Retrieves: Two Component Parts

A blind retrieve is a retrieve that is made when the dog fails to see a bird fall. The handler must point him in the direction of the fall, and the dog, on command, must leave his side, running a line in the direction he was pointed. If he veers from the line, the dog must respond to a single whistle blast by turning to face the handler and sitting down. He then must wait for the handler's directional cast. The dog must not "slip" whistles (that is, fail to respond), and he must not refuse casts, that is, refuse to run in the direction the handler sends him. Thus, there are two component parts to a blind retrieve – *lining* and *handling*.

Blind retrieves occur in numerous circumstances in the field. On a pheasant hunt, for example, you might be working the dog along a brushy fencerow while a line of hunters is scattered across the milo stubble to your right. The field ends at the edge of a creek and as you approach the strip of cover between the edge of the field and the creek, a cock flushes at the far end of the line of hunters. The bird is knocked down and falls across the creek, which is generally the way things go. Naturally, there is no way to get across.

This is the kind of retrieve where your dog earns his keep. If the dog doesn't know how to line and to handle, you might get the bird if you can throw enough rocks in the vicinity of the fall. But there again, the dog might think that playtime has arrived and you might wind up with him bringing your rocks back.

The well-trained retriever, on the other hand, will bring home the meat. But it will take a lot of patience and a lot of work by both of you before you can pick up that bird.

Lining – You started teaching the puppy lining months ago, remember? You strung out the line of bumpers and had him picking them up out to 40 yards or so.

Now you must build on the puppy training. You need to find yet another field in which to train on lining. Don't use the fields where you started the puppy's marking work. Memories of the old falls there might interfere with his work. The lining field can be a vacant lot or a grassy gravel parking lot, anything nice and flat with room to run. Once you've found the field, you will establish a three-legged pattern

95

that, if viewed from above, would look like a crow's foot.

"This is real good," Cotton said, "if you've got a place where you can mow strips, where the dog can see those dummies – a bunch of them. Keep the same number of dummies down each leg where you won't get messed up. I always put mine in separate piles behind me 'cause I get mixed up."

If you have found the field, mow each line of the crow's-foot strips out to about 100 yards. Mowing is not necessary if you find a fresh-cut hayfield or any other mown field. The objective is to have the grass short enough that the pup can sit at your side and see the white bumpers, one behind the other, laying down the lines.

Build one line at a time, starting with the line to the right. Walk about halfway down the mown strip, make the dog sit, then walk to the end of the strip and drop a bumper. Walk back toward the dog, dropping a bumper about every 10 yards. When you get back to the dog, the last bumper you dropped should be about 10 yards away from him. The pup, who has watched you drop the bumpers, will probably line himself up to make the retrieves. If he doesn't, bring him to heel with his head and spine lined up with the bumpers. Take a step toward the bumpers with your left leg if the dog heels on the left. Give him a line by putting the edge of your hand, palm side toward your knee, about a foot in front of his nose and high enough that you do not block his vision. Hold your hand there for a few seconds while he stares at the bumpers. If he looks at your hand, raise it a few inches. He should be looking at the bumpers.

Now "cue" him. After enough repetitions, the cue words will mean "blind retrieve" to the dog. Cotton uses the words "dead bird...dead bird." This also is a good point to start establishing a rhythm with the dog, then stick with it. Through repetition, the rhythm will build in the dog. He will start to lean upon hearing the cue words, expecting to hear the release command on the given beat in the rhythm.

At this point, though, the dog is staring at the bumper 10 yards away. You have cued him with "dead bird," and your hand is down, reinforcing the line. Release him. Use his name, which you have used to release him on marks, and add the word "back." After the dog is going confidently on his lines, you can simply release him with the word "back" if you find it more comfortable. Always use your cue words, though, before the release command.

Use the same procedure to pick up all six bumpers down the line. If the dog is still running well, back up 25 yards and repeat the same drill. Your goal is to move the dog all the way to the end of the right-hand strip and eventually move the bumpers back into a pile at the

Cotton teaches "lining" with this three-legged pattern. He establishes each leg of the pattern by lining up bumpers and sending the dog back and forth until he has picked up each one. Eventually you can move the bumpers closer and closer together until the pup is simply running to a pile of bumpers at the end of each line. (Michael McIntosh Photo)

other end of the strip. When you can get three of four retrieves down the right-hand line, start building the other lines. Eventually you will want a two or three-bumper pile at the end of each line. The number of bumpers will depend on the weather and the conditioning level of your dog. Don't run him into the ground – two or three retrieves down each of the three legs is a good session.

Now that you have the three legs established and the dog is picking up all three bumpers down the right leg, then all three down the middle leg, and finally all three down the left leg, start switching legs. Pick up one down the right leg; then, using the Clock Drill you worked on in obedience training, move him to the left and pick up one from the middle leg. Then go back to the right leg for one, then all the way to the left leg for a bumper. This teaches the dog to follow your leg and go the way your hand points him.

You might have a few problems with this drill when you begin running all three legs. For example, the pup may be sent to one pile and veer toward another. Call him back, walk farther up the original line, and send him again. The bumper you want is closer to him now, and, probably more appealing.

From time to time, you might get a "no go" on this drill. Coax the dog into going. Walk closer to the pile with him, throw a bumper on the pile, and send him. Upon his return, walk farther from the pile and send him again. Work him back down the original starting line.

Try to avoid harsh correction on this drill. Through repetition, he will learn the three legs and this pattern will be good to come back to in the future, when he has gotten into trouble on other training blinds or has otherwise lost confidence. The three-legged pattern should get him going again.

Cotton stressed the importance of the dog learning to trust your line, to believe your hand.

"I think you ought to put your hand down and the dog should go where you line him," Cotton said. "Don't sit up there and let the dog's head wander, lookin' around. Put your hand down there and when he comes in there, release him.

"Give that dog a line to every bird. There's no question about it. Even on marks. Put that hand down on all three birds. It will help you on your blinds. (Releasing the dog without using your hand) Ahh, That's just trying to look, cute. It doesn't look any damn cuter, because if that dog doesn't get that bird out there, he's hurt."

Cotton said that the handler needs to concentrate on giving the dog a good line and then be consistent with his timing and method.

"If he's up there by that knee on your right leg (for a dog that heels on the right), he can't go left if you put that leg out. I don't ever send my dogs with my legs together. This right leg (for his right heelers) is always out. As a rule, it's always pointed pretty much where that bird is. Step right on out with it! Always kind of throw that foot in line with that blind. Send the dog on marks the same way. And then that dog's got confidence when you're putting that hand down too."

When the pup is picking up all the bumpers in any order you want him to, start establishing training blinds or sight blinds for him. Find another field with hunting-type cover, like your marking field. Take one of your bumper throwers with you. Find a high spot in the field from which to run the dog. Locate three good "blinds"; one should be about 40 yards, one about 75, and another about 100 yards. The lines to each blind should involve different lining concepts. For example, maybe there is a patch of cover close to the starting line that the dog has to break through for the 40-yard blind; maybe there is another patch of cover halfway out that he has to run through on the 75-yard blind; maybe there is a ditch the dog has to cross just before he picks up the 100-yard blind. The cover and the ditch are all hunting-type obstacles the dog will have to learn to traverse.

Establish these sight blinds with "marks," and work on them one at a time. Begin by having your bumper thrower plant two or three bumpers where the 40-yard blind will be located. Mark the spot for future reference with a piece of surveyors' tape. Then have him step back and throw a mark at the pile of bumpers. After you pick up the single, send the dog back for the other bumpers. If you get a "no go," encourage him to go by walking toward the pile. If you send him again and he starts to go but slows down, acting confused, signal for your bumper thrower to pitch another bumper for him. In this way you should get him going back to the pile. If he picks up the three bumpers, have your bumper thrower drop three more at the surveyors' tape and then leave the field. Now pick up these bumpers sans gunner. Establish the other two sight blinds in the same manner.

When the dog is going well, which he should in one or two sessions, start working on improving his lines by making the dog drive through the obstacles. You will have to break the lines down into segments. On the middle line, for example, once the dog has learned where the pile of bumpers is, walk up to the edge of the obstacle, the patch of cover, and make him drive straight through. Then gradually work back to your original line. The same should work with the ditch on the 100-yard line.

Cotton adds that the dog's line on his return is as important to your training as his line going out.

"Make him come on back through that cover, too," Cotton said. "Both ways, through the cover. Otherwise, it's making a cheater out of him. What you want to do is move up there close (to the cover) where you can drive him through and you're up there close making him come on straight back to you. Then move on back."

He also suggests using your voice to help the dog drive.

"Very easy on the short one," Cotton said. "'Back'...(normal tone of voice on the 40-yard blind). And on this one I make a very hard 'Back!' (on the 100-yard blind). A very stern voice, to make that dog drive on that line. Tone of voice can be almost as effective as a whip."

Think about what the dog is learning. He is learning that sometimes he finds a bird that he hasn't seen fall at close range, sometimes at slightly longer range, and sometimes at long range; sometimes across a ditch, sometimes through cover close at hand, and sometimes through cover farther away. He also is learning to run off your hand and to develop confidence that when you put your hand down, he is going to get a retrieve.

Repetition is a major part of this phase of training: "If he doesn't do well, go back and do the same thing (the next day)," Cotton said. "I'm a great believer in repetition. That's what I do with the my young dogs. I run on the blind every day for a week. The same blind. They're rolling – I mean diggin'! Some of them, why I mean they'll practically break going to the line."

But, for all your hard work on lining, it's still just half of the blind retrieve. The dog will still have to handle.

Handling – Up to this point, everything you've done with the dog outside of obedience training has relied upon his innate desire to retrieve. Even teaching him to line relied on his desire to pick up those bumpers. Unfortunately, there is nothing about handling that is natural or instinctive to the dog.

Teaching a dog to handle will put your obedience training to the test. Remember when you taught him to sit by your side on the whistle? Now he's going to have to learn to sit whenever you blow that whistle, regardless of where he is.

Cotton said, as a general rule, to start handling training as soon as the dog is through force training and obedience training. But, with an eager learner, younger is even better.

"I start awful young," he said. "If they'll sit and I can throw a dummy to the left and I can throw a dummy to the right and one behind him and make him sit there and get any of those dummies I want, well, he's ready to start handling out in the field. That is, a very aggressive dog, even nine or ten months old."

Cotton starts pups on the same handling drill that professional trainers have been using since the 1940's: the **Baseball Drill**.

The pup sits at the pitcher's mound facing the handler who stands just a few feet away toward home plate. He pitches a bumper to first base, extends his right hand parallel to the ground, holds it in place for a few seconds, and says the dog's name and "over." The dog should pick up the bumper and the handler then meets him at the pitcher's mound where the cast is repeated to third base. When these two casts are done properly, the dog should return to the pitcher's mound, the handler should throw the bumper over the dog's head to second base. Extend the right hand upward, turn the body sideways to the dog, and say his name and "back!"

These are the three casts that a gun dog must answer correctly. As in teaching the dog sight blinds, the dog's name eventually can be dropped prior to the cast. When the dog is taking the casts correctly with one bumper, add another. Throw one to first base and one to third base. If he picks these up successfully, throw a bumper to second base and one to first base. If he picks these up successfully, throw a bumper to second base and one to first base. If he makes a mistake, shout "No," and call him back to the pitcher's mound. Throw a bumper in the direction he should have gone and repeat the cast.

When the pup is doing two bumpers with no mistakes, add a third bumper and always cast him away from the bumper he last saw fall. When the pup returns to the pitcher's mound with a bumper, throw it back to the spot from which it was retrieved and send the pup in another direction. Constantly throwing the bumpers back to their respective bases will tempt the pup to go in that direction. Always cast him away. Before long he will anticipate going the opposite way,

The "baseball drill" – designed to teach the dog hand signals – has been around since the 1940s. Cotton starts a pup with just one bumper and shows him each of the three casts: the cast to first base, the cast to third base, and the cast to second base. The vocal command "over" is used with the casts to first base and third base, and the vocal command "back" is used with the cast to second base. Eventually, the drill is used with the three bumpers in position at once. (Michael McIntosh Photos)

so fool him. Blow the whistle and cast with both arms. That's right, give both a left-hand cast and a right-hand cast at the same time. Then drop one arm to your side, wait a few seconds, and give him the vocal "over." This will prevent the pup from anticipating your cast and breaking as soon as you give the hand signal. Make him wait for the vocal command. Throw this two-handed cast at him now and then just to keep him honest – sort of like showing him the fastball while he's guessing curve.

Smoky learned the baseball drill in just a few days and he began to anticipate the casts. At the least little movement, he was off and running. So Cotton tricks him. He casts with both arms and tells him to "sit." Then he drops one arm and give the vocal command to send Smoky for the bumper. (Michael McIntosh Photos)

Although the Baseball Drill is an important teaching tool, Cotton warns about too much of a good thing:

"Don't overdo it. A lot of dogs think it's a game and they just love it. Some dogs, it gets to be a bore. You give 'em about three different casts, back and over, they get tired or bored and just don't want any part of it. Keep the dog eager and wanting to do it – happy. When you take that out of them, you've overdone it. If he's happy and wants to work, work for 30 minutes. But, like I said, you throw four or five for some dogs and they get to be plodders.

"Now those eager dogs, you have to watch. A lot of them, why as soon as you put that hand up there (the "back" cast), they break. You got to stop that. But then you don't want to get on him too much because he wants to go. So you put him on that check cord again. About 25 feet. Make him sit there and 'toot!' (blow the whistle once, the sit command) and throw that dummy. Jerk him and take him right back there and tell him to sit. Blow that whistle. Everything you do should be straight backs and straight overs. Turning your body sideways (with the hand pointed straight up) is the only way to get a straight back."

At this point, the pup is really good at his casts. Now you need to find out just how good. Go back to your three-legged pattern. Line the dog down each leg. Then set him up to line the middle leg again. Just before he gets to the halfway mark, blow the whistle for him to sit. If he keeps on driving, try it again. If you still don't get the whistle-sit, go back to the truck and get your longest lead, the 50-footer, and the chain collar. Be sure to put on your gloves – heavy gloves.

Set him up and line him down the right-hand leg. When he gets about 15 yards out, blow the sit-whistle and start putting pressure on the rope. A little pressure may be all the reminder he needs. Whatever the cast is, you are going to have to stop him with the lead. If he's a hard driver, you may want to try stopping him even earlier, before he gets a real head of steam up. You may have to go to a longer lead. If you just can't get him to sit on the whistle, leave the three-legged pattern and drill on whistle-sits.

Cotton recommends sitting the dog down, walking away from him maybe 30 or 40 yards, calling him to you, and blowing the whistle when he gets about halfway. A long lead will help on this drill too. You can sit the dog near a sapling or a fence post, run the lead around it, and call the dog. When you blow the sit whistle, clamp down on the lead and you should be able to stop him. Practice this until you can stop the dog three or four times on his return without the lead attached.

Now go back to the three-legged pattern. Send him down the middle leg and blow the sit whistle. When he stops, cast him to the pile at the end of the right-hand leg. He may be confused and start to go, stop, and look at you. Keep casting and coaxing him. You may have to cast him several times, but keep moving in the direction of the right-hand pile and when you cast, move your arm from the elbow to the wrist in a waving motion. You want to make sure he can see the cast. Upon his return, send him all the way down the middle leg. Now send him back down the middle leg, stop him and cast again to the right-hand pile. The results should be better this time. Eventually, make the dog sit and cast from each leg. Be sure to throw a few straight-up back casts in there from time to time.

When the retriever understands the casts off the baseball drill, go back to your three-legged lining pattern and combine the two drills. Send the dog down the middle leg, stop him with a single whistle blast, and cast him to the bumpers at the end of the right-hand leg. You may have to cast several times to get him to the pile. Keep blowing that whistle and casting. Be patient. (Michael McIntosh Photo)

Next, send the dog down the right-hand leg and try a cast to the left, toward the middle leg. You may have to stop him a second time on this maneuver and cast him back to the pile. (Michael McIntosh Photo)

Then send the dog down the middle leg and try another cast to the left. (Michael McIntosh Photo)

Finally, send the dog down the middle leg and cast him straight back. Keep in mind that after you stop the dog and cast him on one of the legs, you need to send him all the way through on that leg when he comes in. (Michael McIntosh Photo)

Cotton said that one of the problems you will eventually run into on this drill is the "pop," that is the dog will stop and wait for a cast without hearing a whistle. This often is caused by anticipation. The dog has been sent, stopped, and cast on this pattern for several weeks.

"You've got certain spots out there to stop him," Cotton said. "It's a good idea to have a man out there on a young dog. If he sees the dog is gonna stop without the whistle, he should holler 'Hey, hey, pup!' and throw a dummy (at the pile). Let him roll. Then you turn around and let him roll all the way again. Next time, you stop him and make him go left or right, whichever way you want to. When you're doing this, have those dummies where they dog can see 'em. If you don't, you're gonna get a dog that does a lot of poppin'.'"

Generally speaking, a sensitive dog will be more apt to pop. He wants to please and he knows it pleases you when he stops and casts. This is not a bad reaction for a hunting dog. It's better than the opposite, the hard-headed dog that runs around like an idiot, refusing to stop and cast.

Which brings up another problem you might see on this pattern work – coasting on the whistle. You will blow the whistle and the dog will slow down gradually, make a big turn, and eventually sit down. If you let this slide, before long the dog will be riding right through your whistle – he won't stop at all, so nip the "coaster" in the bud.

"You've got to make him put it down," Cotton said. "Go out there and get ahold of him. Tear him up. If he's hard to catch, run him with a rope on him. It makes a difference on age. If it's a young dog, don't get too rough on him. Pop him back to you a time or two with the rope. Then send him, stop him, and call him all the way back. Then send him out there and stop him at 20 feet and throw another dummy to your right and make him get it.

"With the older dog, you catch him, blow that whistle, and shake the hell out of him. Blow that whistle and tell him to 'sit!, sit!' And, if you have to, flip him with a fifty-foot rope once, if he's really hard-headed. Have someone throw another dummy, send him, hit the whistle, and if he doesn't stop, flip him. You're doing a lot of force training there, so repeat him again and let him go all the way. Don't ever finish up with a jerk like that, let him make one or two retrieves free. You better have a pair of gloves on, now, when you do that."

The goal is to be able to send the dog down any of the three lines, stop him with the whistle, and handle him to any of the piles. Cotton recommends that you always handle "on the square." That means when you stop the dog on the right leg of the pattern and you want to pick up a bumper from the middle pile, cast him left onto the line to the middle pile, stop him again with the whistle, and cast him straight back to the bumper. Don't let the dog scallop back on his casts. In other words, "over" means *over*, not *over and back*. If you let the dog get into the habit of going over and then angling back, before long you won't be able to get a true "over."

When the pup is lining and casting well on the three-legged pattern, start stopping him and casting him on the three sight blinds mentioned earlier. Line him to the 100-yard blind beyond the ditch, stop him and handle him to the 75-yard blind, and so on.

The pup should be putting it all together by now – the lining and casting. So try him on a simple "cold" blind retrieve – a blind retrieve he has never done. Don't set up a blind with any tough obstacles. Maybe it's just 60 yards across a cow pasture.

By this time, the pup is so conditioned to go on "back" that you should have no trouble getting him away from your side. But he may just go 10 or 15 yards and start to wander, maybe even check back with you. If so, stop him with the whistle and handle him. Eventually, you should be able to hack him to the bumper. Don't give up as long as he is answering your whistle commands. If he stops sitting on the whistle, catch him and immediately go through your "whistle-sit" drill on the spot. You will be closer to the bumper by this time, and you should be able to hack him the rest of the way to complete the retrieve.

In this early going, one or two easy cold blinds a week will be plenty. And, after you have run them once, you will automatically have more memory blinds that you can repeat in the future. When you repeat the blinds, though, try to get them in fewer whistles than you did the time before. Eventually the dog should "line" them, that is pick the bumper up without handling.

You now have reached a level of training where your actions as a handler are as important to the outcome of the retrieve as the dog's abilities. Every so often you will stumble onto the blind retrieve where one wrong cast at the right time will make the retrieve practically impossible. Try to see your own actions through the eyes of the dog. Always keep in mind that the dog has built-in weaknesses, like casting into the wind.

"He won't want to cut into that wind," Cotton said. "There's no dog that likes to cast into the wind. They don't like to, but you want to practice on that too. I run all my young dogs into the wind a lot."

That way, when you need that cast in a hunting situation, you might just get it.

During training, keep your mind working. Can the dog see your cast? Is your cast confusing to him, halfway between an over and a back? Is your timing bad? Did your last cast put the dog behind cover where he cannot be seen? At this point, you and the dog have to become a team. You have to understand each other. Be consistent with your handling and be consistent with your training – you can't let the dog take bad casts in training and then expect to get good casts in a hunting situation. If anything, handling will get looser during the hunt. So the more consistent and structured you are in training, the better the results are going to be in the duck blind.

Training Avenues

Basically, the retriever's land training involves marked retrieves, lining, handling, and blind retrieves. Cotton suggests thinking of these training elements as converging avenues, all meeting at the same point – the finished retriever.

Cotton works on all of these training elements concurrently. In other words, one day he works on marks, the next day he runs the three-legged pattern with casts, the next day he teaches the lines to a couple of sight blinds, then another day he runs a pair of "cold" blinds. Eventually, Cotton points out, you will be able to combine the training. For instance, if you have a triple mark set up and the dog forgets the third bird and starts to go into an old fall, you simply show him the way to the proper fall by handling him, then repeat the mark as a single.

Eventually, when the dog understands sight blinds and is marking well, you will be able to combine the two much the way Cotton did with Smoky at the beginning of this chapter.

But be on guard. There are pitfalls, especially if your training leans too heavily on handling and blind retrieves.

"I would train about equally (on handling and marking). But that goes back to individual dogs too, you know. It's going to bother a young dog's marking if you do quite a bit of handling on him," Cotton said. "It's going to mess his marking up just a little bit."

Cotton added that too much handling can result in other marking problems too, such as giving up the hunt and turning to you for help. When that happens, Cotton advises against handling him to the bird or bumper.

"More marks and don't handle him on those marks. If nothing else, have a bird boy help him out. Or walk him into it," Cotton said. "Never handle on marks, no, if the dog has a tendency to 'pop' on marks. Have that man take him into the fall. Then repeat him on a single right back to that same place. He'll start staying out there and hunting. I think this indicates he's been handled too much. I'd forget about blinds with him for awhile. Leave off the blinds. Definitely leave off combination marks and blinds. Straight marks or straight blinds. If you handle him on marks a lot, depending on the dog, he's going to start looking for it."

Ultimately, when the dog has learned to handle and is running his "cold" blinds with confidence, your training should be at a level where you try to show the dog different hunting situations. The typical training session operates like this:

It's Saturday morning. You assemble a training group and head to the nearest state-operated wildlife area. The group decides to work on a land triple that simulates a pheasant drive. You work your dog through the triple, eventually reaching a satisfactory result. Maybe you had to repeat only one mark. You trade places with one of the bird throwers and he takes his turn training. After everyone has worked on the land triple, the group decides to set up a blind retrieve in the same field, this too is typical of a hunting situation, that is, going back across old falls to pick up a bird the dog has not seen fall.

At this level – maybe the dog is getting close to two-years old - drill work will be used only sparingly, whenever the dog needs a confidence-builder.

If you run into trouble in a training situation, simplify. Show the dog what you want and repeat it. Remember, repetition is your most important training tool.

Cotton waves at his two grandbabies.

"Mandy! You and D.J. come on in now. We're done here."

Cotton puts his foot up on the bumper of his pickup.

"You need to train with birds whenever you can," he said. "When I was working at Nilo, we trained with birds about every day."

He pulls a bandana out of his hip pocket, removes his long-billed fishing cap, and wipes the sweat from his brow.

"Startin' to heat up. Let's go down the road and do a water blind and some marks. That spring water down there is cold and clean. It's beautiful, now, just beautiful!"

He loads kids, bumpers, and dogs and heads down the road.

Chapter Five

WATER RETRIEVES: MARKS AND BLINDS

The wind was blowing out of the north, so Cotton drove to the far end of the big marsh. He parked the truck near a huge concrete drain that, long ago, controlled the flow of water out of the marsh and under the road, back in the days when the marsh had been used as a fish hatchery. Beavers now kept the drain plugged with willow cuttings and mud.

The marsh looked like an ideal place for a duck shoot, and as Cotton slammed the door of the pickup, a pair of wood ducks flushed from the heavy growth of willows and cattails growing at the edge of the old creek channel where the marsh ran up against a hillside covered with a dense stand of oaks and hickories.

"Isn't this beautiful?" Cotton asked, grinning, hands on his hips. He rummaged through the training gear in the back of the truck again and produced a pair of orange bumpers.

"All right," Cotton said to Mandy and D.J. "You two get your bumpers. Mandy, you walk up the levee there and throw your bumper right out in the middle. D.J., you go to the left and throw across that little cut of water there so the bumper falls on the other side of that little strip of land, okay?"

Cotton walked down the left shoreline and disappeared into the brush. Moments later he appeared about a 100 yards away where the old creekbed bent to the west into the marsh. He dropped his bumper at the bend and headed back. The two orange bumpers shined like twin beacons at the end of the channel, lined on one side by the heavily timbered ridge and on the other by a heavy growth of willows. Cotton opened Smoky's crate and let him "air."

"Now, I'm going to run this blind first," Cotton said. "Smoky's run it quite a few times so I shouldn't have any trouble with it. I put that other bumper out just in case I need to repeat him on it. Then we'll do the double. Working in this spring water is the only way to train when it's hot. It's no good training on land in the heat of the day. You get a dog hot, real hot, and he doesn't even know what he's doin'. It's hard on 'em."

Cotton lined Smoky up just as he did on the land work. He took a step forward with his right leg and put his hand down; Smoky coiled, muscles quivering. On command, the dog launched himself into the water. He swam straight down the channel, slipped just past the two bumpers, but caught the wind right and hooked back to them.

Cotton explained the importance of teaching the dog this channel concept. He said the dog's natural tendency is to run the edge, to run the bank. When he learns the channel concept, his thinking shifts. Instead of thinking land, he thinks "water."

He added that the most important work a retriever does is in the water, and if his thinking isn't weighted that way, he may have difficulty picking up those difficult marks and blinds from the duck boat.

The same thinking applies to water work as applied in the lining drills through cover on land. The dog should maintain straight lines to his marks. He stands a lot better chance of making a successful retrieve if he goes directly out and back. If you let him "cheat," that is run the bank to pick up his birds, the next thing you know, he won't get in the water at all, especially on blind retrieves or when there's a skim of ice.

Cotton drove this point home when he told of a hunting situation that occurred in 1984 on Truman Lake. The hunting party had spotted a few ducks on a creek that wound through a stand of timber on the Grand River arm of the reservoir. Two of the hunters plotted a jump shooting strategy and slipped into the timber, quickly out of sight of the other two members of the hunting party.

About 15 minutes had passed when five shots rang out. Hundreds of ducks, from every little pocket of water in the timber, leaped into the air. There were shouts from the timber: "Bring the dogs! Bring the dogs!"

The two hunters who had stayed behind went into action, releasing two Labrador retrievers and heading into the timber to help the others collect their birds. Five ducks, all greenheads, had gone down. Two had fallen on the hunter's side of the creek and were already in hand. Two more were slowly drifting down the creek, belly up, and the fifth duck had fallen across the creek, not 40 yards away in a heap of brush and debris.

The older of the two dogs, a five-year-old female, ran to the edge of the creek, saw the ducks drifting, jumped in, and quickly brought one of the two birds to hand. The younger dog ran down the bank, chasing the second, current-driven bird. His handler went with him, shouting encouragement.

The hunters finally managed to pick up the other duck in the debris with the old female, an experienced duck dog. It wasn't pretty – they had finally coaxed the dog across the creek by throwing rocks. She was lucky enough to hit the bank in a spot where she winded the bird.

Then they heard the ruckus downstream – profanity that would make a sailor blush. The hunters raced down the bank just in time to see a big-eyed black dog go careening into the water. He landed on his side, facing the bank, the result of a two-handed, underarmed sling – not expected ever to be an Olympic event.

The dog immediately swam back to the bank where a sweating, cursing owner stood ready to do him great physical harm. The dog thought better of landing as he got closer to the bank and finally decided to stand, belly deep in the mud, wagging his tail.

"Where's the duck?"

"Over there," the hunter said. Panting, he pointed to the far bank where the duck had hung up in a root wad. "B.J.! You #%^&, come here!"

B.J. the dog decided that standing in the cold, muddy water was a better alternative. Finally, when the hunters coaxed the old female into the creek, B.J. decided to join her and the two swam across. B.J. conceded the duck.

Training is the only way to create dependability in a retriever. Even the old female in this story would have performed better if she had been taught to line and to handle.

The hours spent training will greatly reduce the frustration level of the hunt.

Water Marks

Smoky watched intently as Cotton called for the marks. The first bumper thrown landed with a splash about 75 yards out behind a table-sized clump of cattails; the second bumper went behind a long spit of land about 40 yards to the dog's left. There were two lining concepts involved: The first required the dog to angle into the water and drive through the cattails, and the second required the dog to get into the water, cross the spit, and re-enter the water to pick up the bumper. Smoky nailed both marks.

The same basic elements are common to land marks and water marks: The dog must be steady so he can see the falls, he must go on command, run a line to the area of the fall, hunt the area thoroughly, then return and deliver the bird gently to hand.

All the problems you dealt with in the dog's land work will seem like minor annoyances compared to the ones you will deal with in water work, mainly because the dog is infinitely more difficult to reach. When you begin water training, wait for warm water, even if you have to wait six months. Let the dog ease into working in cold water. Your chances of creating a good water attitude are much better when the dog's started in warm water.

Beginning water marks should concentrate on creating a good attitude and good style.

"Don't give him any long retrieves,"Cotton said. "Short retrieves. Put a flappin' duck out there or a (clipped-wing) pigeon, no more than 30 or 40 feet. Tell him 'back,' and hit him with a switch – just a little bit. (If you're doing blinds) Do all sight blinds with him and stay away from those long blinds in the water."

Cotton said style, no matter how hard you work on getting the dog to hit the water hard, is generally a matter of the individual dog's personality.

"This golden (retriever) I trained once, his name was Golden Kid," Cotton said. "You get him in a small body of water, there wasn't very many dogs in the United States that would beat him. But you get him out on a big body of water, like a big lake where you had a floating blind or some long marks, you know, or a boat out there or something. God Almighty, he'd go out there and he'd trot in. Kinda piggish. I mean, it just wasn't like the Golden Kid. But now you get him on a small body of water, like a little pond. He'd rare back and he'd try to jump it, it seemed like, he'd hit the water so hard."

You will need to add a switch to your bag of training tools. A riding crop works well or, if you find yourself constantly losing these store-bought sticks, just whack an appropriate branch off a hickory tree.

If your pup is working well on single land marks, if he has been introduced properly to the water as a puppy, and if the weather and water temperature are cooperative, get him wet. As with the rest of the work you've done, start simple. Stand with the pup at the very edge of a pond and have your bumper thrower go down the bank a few yards to your left. Upon command, have him shout or shoot the blank pistol and throw a bumper. The bumper should land about 10 yards out, directly in front of you. Send the dog as soon as the bumper splashes, just as you would on a land mark. If the dog responds properly, have your thrower pitch the next bumper directly in front of you but about 20 yards out. Gradually work the dog on longer and longer retrieves until he is going as far as the thrower can throw.

Keep in mind, all of these retrieves are done "on the square," that is straight out from the bank. The bumper should land in open water, in plain sight of the dog. Keep sending him from the water's edge. The dog also has been forced to retrieve at this point so make him finish up properly, just like he does on land. In the beginning, he may drop the bumper and shake as soon as his feet touch bottom. Command "fetch," and from this point on, tell him to "hold" as soon as he gets into shallow water. Also command "heel." You may have to use a lead and a few short, handler-thrown retrieves to make him come directly to heel. Keep on him – you may have to pinch his ear a few times to make your commands stick, but don't give up.

If the dog is steady on land, the chances are good that he is going to be even steadier when it comes to water marks. But always be prepared for the break. For the first few retrieves, keep that short rope lead, slack, in your right hand.

If the pup was introduced to the water properly and if he is an eager retriever and the water is comfortably warm, you shouldn't get into a no go problem – yet. The no go problem will come later. Rest assured, though, whether it's sooner or later, it will happen.

Now that the dog is going as far as your assistant can throw in open water, add another bumper, a handler-thrown. It goes like this: The assistant throws his bumper into open water, visible to the dog from the line and a retrieve that he has made before. Then you, the handler, pitch one close, just a few feet to the right. The pup should pick up your mark and then go for the longer mark, the mark that he has been picking up as a single.

You can start training these short water doubles as soon as the pup is doing land doubles. The purpose of this exercise is to get the pup going as soon as possible for a mark that he has to remember. You are conditioning him to go on command.

At this point, you will probably be able to determine just what you are working with in the way of the pup's natural abilities. If, at this point, after the pup has been through the forced retrieve and he isn't showing interest and never has, you should be considering another dog, because the training from this point on becomes more stressful, more demanding – the puppy days are over, and the real retriever work has begun. It is absolutely necessary that the dog have a high level of desire both to please you and to retrieve.

After the pup is comfortable with retrieving from the water, he will need to learn that sometimes he has to get out on the far bank to find a bird. So start the pup with a mark in the water. If he retrieves successfully, make the next mark up against the bank on the same line he swam on the first mark. The third bumper should be thrown several yards up the bank, again on the same line the pup has been swimming. Do not let the pup "cheat," that is run around the bank to pick up the bumper.
(Michael McIntosh Photos)

Training a good, working retriever – one that will mark, line, and handle well enough to be an asset rather than a hindrance in the field – requires a great deal of work with a good dog. With a poor dog, it is all but impossible.

Nevertheless, with just a little coaxing, the pup will start picking up these short doubles. Now you need to get him onto land at the far end of the retrieve. This means your assistant needs to be on one bank of a pond, you and the dog on the other. Have the assistant start out by throwing a mark angled slightly toward you into the water. Big splash. The pup retrieves. The next mark should be on the same line, but land right *at* the water's edge. The pup swims across the small pond and picks the bumper up and returns. Now you need to get his feet dry. Have the assistant throw the third bumper up on the bank, where the pup has to come out of the water to pick it up.

By throwing the shorter bumpers, you should have taught the pup that the correct line was out and back in the water. But when he gets his feet dry, he might look down the bank and decide that's a much better way of getting back. If this is the result, your work has begun. To avoid this, as soon as the pup picks up the bumper, start blowing your whistle and calling him. If he starts to go down the bank, immediately shout "No!" and give it the emphasis you need. If the dog persists, blow the sit whistle. If you get the proper response, go to him, take him back to the spot where he picked up the bumper, take the bumper from him, and pitch it on the proper line back into the water. Walk around to the starting point and call him to you. You may have to tell him to fetch as well. Now he has to get in the water to pick up the bumper and get back.

The appropriate body of water can make this marking/lining drill much simpler. Working across a channel, the short way, will discourage cheating. Working across a creek (little or no current) also will keep him honest. Finally, you may have to resort to a lead, tugging him gently back into the water on the return.

The assistant, at this point, can help too. When the pup picks up the bumper, the assistant can try to haze or herd the pup back into the water. Be careful with this maneuver, though. The last thing you want the assistant to do is spook the pup. One bad experience could make him forever shy of gunners in the field. Proceed gently, Cotton advises.

"You got to watch it now," Cotton said. "I had a man workin' for me one time, I told him to get this one dog. I said make him come back by the water. Get after him. I said pick up a little switch or something and get after him. Well, there was a log laying there, about three inches in diameter, and he grabbed that thing, about six-foot long, and he came down on the water.

"I said, 'Don't kill him! I got to run him in the national (retriever championship) in three days.' He was a tough dog. It didn't bother him, he went on back (for the mark). I did it right then. If I hadn't done it a time or two after that, though, that dog could have been shy. When you start a problem like that, I think you got to finish it out."

At this point in training, don't tempt the dog to cheat by making him angle into the water, but you can start lengthening the entry. Once you have the pup successfully swimming across the pond, getting out and picking up the mark then returning by water, back up from the edge of the water about 10 yards.

At this point, you might get a balk, especially on the second bird of a double. This is the way it will happen: The mark will go down across the pond, then you will throw a bumper into the water. The pup will pick up the last bird down and return. You will set him up to pick up the long mark, one he has done as a single many times, and when you send him he will run to the water's edge and stop. He might even turn around and look at you.

Give him another chance. Call him back, line him up again and send him. If he fails to get in the water this time, you need to use the whip. Grab his short rope lead and give him about three swats with the switch while commanding "back!" or whatever word you have decided to use as a command to send the dog. Set him down right at the water's edge and send him again. He should go.

On a hardcase, you may have to put a choke chain on him and run a lead across the pond and while you switch him, have the person on the other bank pull him into the water. As soon as he gets wet, toss a bumper in the water for him. Again, you are reinforcing the attitude that the water is the best place to be. As soon as the dog gets wet and picks up the bumper, praise him, then repeat the mark as a single.

You are going to get this balking problem from time to time in your training. Be consistent with your correction and never end your training session with a balk. Get the dog going again before you put him back in the crate.

Continue moving back with your starting point, always keeping the entry square across the pond. When he does this properly, have the thrower move back until the mark is falling well back from the water's edge, maybe 20 yards. When the pup is making this retrieve – the long entry into the water, the mark well up the bank – without balking or cheating (trying to run around the pond), you're making progress.

"I used to do a lot of that at Nilo," Cotton said. "I'd get way back here, I'd get back, oh, maybe a hundred yards. And I'd put them down and they would have to go up and over, back, across a road, over a dam, and get on in the water. The lake ran way down into a cove. The shorelines had a lot of suction. This was a good repetition blind. You had to start right up on the dam with the young dog. Anytime you have a young dog, you got to show him something like this and then start backing up. And always show him with a mark."

Keep in mind, when you back up from the water, the pup is going to have to hold the bumper all the way to heel before he can shake. Demand this. Keep on the whistle as soon as he gets out of the water on the return and reinforce vocally if necessary.

Once he comes all the way to heel, take the bumper and let him shake off. Try to turn this into a habit; he shouldn't shake until he has delivered. Eventually, by holding up on the short rope lead when you take the bumper, you can prevent him shaking until you release the pressure. When you release the pressure, add the command, "shake." Eventually the dog will wait after he delivers until he gets the command. This is especially helpful in the duck blind. You can make him shake outside the blind, keeping equipment inside the blind dry.

Now add another mark to the drill. By this time, through repetition alone, the pup should be going strongly on the second bird and you can start making his water marks longer, that is, making the swims longer. Remember, before throwing the pup a double water mark, give him the two marks as singles.

Marking Drills

The following are two drills, both doubles, that will hone your dog for the duck season. When he gets these drills down pat, he's ready to go hunting.

Swim-By Double Drill – This drill is comparable to the In-Line Triple drill you did on land. Only two marks will be used on this one, though.

Begin with two gunners on the far side of a pond about 50 yards apart. The starting point should be square to these gunners, that is, both marks are at about the same distance from the dog. Both marks should be thrown either to the left or to the right. Do them as singles and then, if the dog picks them up with no problems, make it a double. When you get this square double down, move your starting point down the bank so that one mark is now shorter than the other. The marks are still thrown in the same places, you have just moved to change the angle of the lines to the falls. This will be much more difficult. Again, start with singles.

The Swim-By Double Drill: Try to find a piece of water where you can start this drill "square," which means the gunners would be at an equal distance to you. First pick up the two marks as singles. When the dog will successfully do the singles, try the double. Call for the right-hand mark, then the left-hand mark, and send the dog. The object of the drill is to teach the dog to mark an area across a body of water and to stay in that area until he picks up the bird or bumper. Your gunners must be alert to the dog trying to switch areas or switch birds. Have them help him out immediately with another bumper. Don't let the dog cheat the bank or switch falls. When the dog has mastered this drill on the square, tighten the lines to the marks by moving down the bank. Again, don't let him cheat or switch falls. (Michael McIntosh Photo)

"Anytime you get across a little body of water with any kind of angle at all," Cotton said, "anytime you get two birds across one little body of water, it's touchy. What they'll generally want to do is cut back toward the short bird, the one they've already picked up. And, if they go ahead and get by that fall, they'll go in too short of the second bird and start to hunt and before you know it, they're lost. What you need to do is handle to that lost bird (the second bird) and then repeat it as a single. There ain't no shortcuts.

"Another thing you can do is first give the dog the double as single marks a couple of times, then treat both marks as sight blinds. You got to be careful about correction on this type of training. If you call them back a lot off the marks and reline them, then they'll start thinking that they're leaving a mark and going on a blind. Then, the next thing you know, they quit hunting altogether and start popping a lot, just waiting for you to handle them."

This is a difficult concept for the dog. Don't let him cheat by landing short on the longer of the two marks. Cheating here will probably get him into trouble, as Cotton pointed out.

By-A-Point and Over-A-Point – At the same time, you will need to find a pond with a long point or spit protruding into the water.

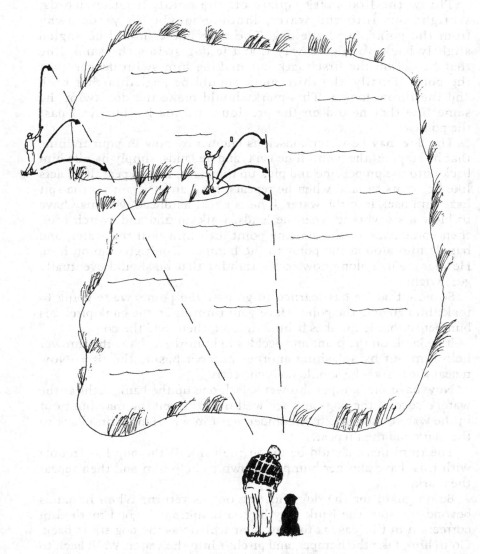

"By-A-Point and Over A Point." Plan on spending many training sessions teaching the dog these marks. This is advanced work, but typical of the marks a dog might get in a hunting situation. If he has been trained successfully on these marks, he is more likely to pick up similar tough marks in a hunting situation. (Art by Christopher Smith)

121

Position one gunner far out on the point, throwing a mark to a spot where the dog has to swim on a line just past the point. Position the second gunner down the bank, throwing a mark that splashes in the pocket of water behind the spit. To train on these two marks effectively, the dog needs to be handling!

Throw the first mark square off the point. In other words, straight out into the water, landing maybe 10 yards away from the point. Send the dog. The next mark should be angled slightly back, in such a way that the dog swims the same line that he did on the first mark but making him swim deeper, past the point. Finally, the third mark should be angled farther back and the throw longer. This mark should make the dog swim the same line that he did on the previous two marks, but well past the point.

The dog may be water-conscious enough by now in your training that he stays off the point. If he isn't, and he lands, simply handle him back onto the proper line and pick up the mark, then repeat. If he acts like he wants to land when he repeats, have an assistant on the spit haze him back into the water. If he is a real hardhead, you may have to blow a sit whistle when he lands, walk around and switch him, then come back to the starting point, call him into the water, and handle him around the point to the bumper. Don't give up on him. He's far enough along now in his training that he should eventually get it right.

So now that he has learned to go past the point, we're going to make him go *over* the point. Have your thrower on the bank pitch his bumper so that it splashes behind the spit, then send the dog.

If he lands on the point and decides to hunt there, have the thrower help him out by splashing another bumper beside the first. Now repeat the mark – he should do it correctly.

Now have the bumper thrower splash one up the bank, right at the water's edge. If the dog can't see well over the spit, he may hunt out in the water where the first bumper was thrown. Handle him back to the mark and then repeat.

The third mark should be up on the bank. If the pup has trouble with this, have another bumper thrown to help him and then repeat the mark.

Be on guard for the dog cheating on his return. When he lands beyond the spit, the bank may be too tempting. A good method of correction in this case is to blow a sit whistle as the dog starts back. Go to him, take the bumper, and pitch it into the water. Walk back to the starting point and give the dog an "over" to get into the water and pick up the bumper, and repeat the mark. He may cheat again on his return, going down the bank to the point where you blew the sit whistle before he gets in. Be ready. When it looks like this will be his tactic, blow the sit whistle again, walk out to him, switch him, take the bumper and pitch it in, go back to the starting point, and handle him into the water. He should get it right on the next repeat. Get these two marks down perfectly as singles before trying to combine them as a double.

Blind Retrieves

Water blinds, like land blinds, involve lining and handling. And, like land blinds, you need to drill on both elements of the blind retrieve.

You will have a more advanced dog to work with on these drills, thanks to your land work. You know how to set up sight blinds, and the dog has been through the Baseball Drill so he understands the three casts. Before starting on these water drills, though, the pup should be lining and casting on his three-legged land pattern.

Go back to the pond where you taught the dog to get into the water and out again to pick up a mark. That mark will now become a sight blind. Start off as you did on land. Plant several bumpers where you were running the mark, have an assistant throw a mark at the pile, and send the dog. Upon his return, line him up just as you did in the land work. If he's a left-side heeler, step forward with the left foot, tell him "dead bird" and "back." He's done this line as a mark enough times that he should get it as a sight blind with no problem.

Now you are going to create another sight blind. As mentioned earlier, a channel or creek will work best for this. If a round pond is all you have access to, you can make it work, but it will require more sweat and more pressure on the dog.

Have the assistant who helped set up the first sight blind move to the right about 50 yards and throw a mark at such a spot that the dog will have to run at an angle to the water's edge, cut into the water, and swim on the same angle to exit on the other side. On a round pond, the line to this mark should slice a piece off one corner of the pond.

If the pup angles in, angles across, and picks up the mark, you have dodged the bullet. More than likely, he will run to the water's edge, slide down the bank, and eventually "square" across. If you're using a round pond, he might not get wet at all, continuing around to the right. Don't settle for this. The dog is stopping on the whistle at this point in his training, so stop him. Call him back and take him on the proper line to the water's edge. Repeat the mark and send him again.

"Put him across there where he can't get in a problem of running

When teaching the dog to angle down a bank into the water, Cotton often simplifies the process by pitching a line of bumpers across the corner of a pond. Handle this as if you were doing one of the legs on your three-legged lining pattern. The line of bumpers will teach him the angle, but when he gets out on the other side, be ready to correct him for "cheating" on the return. (Michael McIntosh Photo)

around," Cotton said. "I'd get right up there, right where he had to get in. If nothing else, I'd slip that little twenty-five-foot rope on him and if he started going around again, I'd yank his head back and I'd put it down there again and make him go. So then you make him get in there that way and then you move back. Give him a mark and then turn around and have the thrower put another one or two of them out for a blind and then put him on out there. Don't worry about going on with anything else until you get that dog going straight over and straight back – not until he quits trying to cheat."

Cotton adds that the most important correction you can make is on his return line: "The most important thing is to get somebody after that dog to make him come back straight," Cotton said. (Have someone other than the bumper thrower standing near the water's edge to haze the dog into the water.) "That's where you're going to get things conquered real quick. You see, if you make him go across there (on the way to the bumper) and then he runs around (on the return trip), that makes it much harder to go back in there straight again. If you make him come back two or three times straight, then you got it licked."

So now you have two water blinds – sight blinds – that you can come back and run from time to time. One sends the dog on about a 10-yard entry to the water, square in, across, and up a bank on the other side; the other sends the dog on an angle in and back out.

Create at least one more sight blind that will make the dog swim down a channel. An assistant should throw a mark to set up this sight blind the same way the other two sight blinds were created. The temptation to run the bank both ways, that is, both going and coming in, will be great, so you will need to get a person on each shoreline to help you keep the dog in the water. Your "hazers" should keep the dog actually swimming, not walking in the water next to the bank. By teaching him this channel concept, you are reinforcing his thinking that the water is the best place to be.

If you don't have the help you need to keep the dog in the water, handle him. Line the dog from the water's edge, right down the channel. If he tries to skirt, say "no!" emphatically and call him back. He has to go straight into the water. If he gets in and starts to angle toward one of the closer shorelines, handle him. Hack him all the way to the end and keep him wet. If he lands, which means he has refused casts, set him down with the whistle after he has refused to cast back into the water, walk down the bank, and give him a few swats with your switch. Step back and cast him into the water and handle him to the bumper.

If he tries to cheat on the return, stop him with the whistle, walk down the bank, pitch the bumper back into the channel, go back to your original starting point, and cast him in. You might have to repeat this type of correction until the dog swims all the way back to the starting point. Repeat the channel blind. It is important to point out that when the dog is finally doing this channel blind correctly, don't think that you will be able to take him to another channel and get the same results; you might, and you might not. You have to be prepared to make the necessary corrections whenever you train, so don't let your guard down. Eventually you will be able to look at a retrieve, whether it is in training or in a hunting situation, and pretty much know what your dog will do. This way you can prepare yourself for the correction.

There is never, really, a point where you can say: "I won't have to train this dog to stay in the water anymore. He's broke." It never really happens, because if you relax one day and let him take a little more of the bank going in or coming back, then the next time he will run just a little bit more bank and so on, until – that's right – he's running around. This is especially true when training on channels.

"This training is all well and good," you say, "but I don't care if he runs the bank, so long as he picks up my ducks!"

Suffice it to say, you just can't have it both ways; the dogs just aren't built like that. They are opportunists and they will take advantage of every break you give them. And duck hunting is the most difficult of the retriever's work because you don't bring the dog along to pick up the ducks that fall dead in the decoys, you bring him along to pick up those difficult birds – the cripples, the birds that fall back into the flooded timber where the boat can't go and where the wading is tough.

The dog *has* to handle and he *has* to get in the water, stay in the water, and pick up those birds. So in training, get determined – don't quit until he's doing the water work correctly.

Handling In Water

Now you are teaching the dog water marks and sight blinds involving three different concepts. You need to add a handling drill in the water to your training. A round pond will work.

You will need two assistants to begin this drill. Start off at the edge of the water and have one assistant across the pond throw a single so that the line to the bumper is straight across the pond. Send the dog to pick up the single.

"Do it again," Cotton said, "but this time stop him, 'toot' (halfway across the pond) and cast him over. Signal the other assistant (standing on the shore to your right) and have him throw a bumper so the dog takes the cast. Keep the bumper in the water. Then send him out there again (for the original mark), maybe let him get that one and come back. Throw the mark again, send him, and 'toot,' 'over!' and then don't let the thrower throw right away, maybe you have to give him two or three casts, see, to the right then you finally give him the bumper – a white bumper, have it thrown where he can see it. Work this drill to the other side too, always in straight lines, everything you do, straight backs and straight overs."

With this drill, the configuration of the pond is not so important. On the other hand, if you are on your own doing this training, Cotton said establish a three-legged pattern much like you did in the land work. Do one leg at a time. Length is not as important as making the dog stop in the water and cast. You begin by throwing bumpers in a line across the right corner of the pond until you get one on the bank. Start picking up bumpers, which shows the dog the proper line to take to what will become a pile of bumpers on the bank.

Do this for the middle leg and the left-hand leg. When the pup is lining all three legs, just like in the land work, start stopping him and casting. Again, you may need to use a long lead to prevent coasting or a big, looping turn on the whistle. You also may need an assistant to throw a bumper now and then to get a cast. This is a good drill to run through decoys. Throw a dozen into the pond after the pup is lining to the three piles and taking his casts.

"After you work a dog through decoys," Cotton said, "he isn't going to bother them. If he acts interested, tell him 'no,' and handle him on to the pile."

Although Cotton has an aversion to training that relies too heavily on mechanical help or force, on problem casts he has resorted in the past to a technique that both forces the dog into the water and forces him to cast.

"If you want to force them to handle in the water, you put a check cord on one side of the collar and another check cord on the other side of the collar," Cotton said. "You have a man over there on the far bank holding one check cord and another person on your side holding the other check cord. So you've got a rope attached to that dog both ways. Now you don't have to have a big wide piece of water. More like a long channel is the best. You need a good man over on the other side that knows how to jerk when you tell him to jerk.

"So you send that dog out, say give him a mark. You send that dog right then, but then, halfway across you go 'toot,' and you hit him with a 'right over' and he's gonna wheel and scallop back because you just threw a mark over there. 'Toot!' over! But he scallops again. All right, now, the next 'toot' you cast him right and he's got to go right, because the man over there, that man's got him, see. He's got him. And you take him right on down the channel where you have a pile of bumpers on the bank. Then you bring him back and take him right on down the left side the same way."

This is where it is important to use ski rope. Ski rope will float, which prevents tangling in submerged brush and debris. This also is a good point to introduce diversions, which means you will teach the dog to go where you send him regardless of the distractions.

Use your three-legged water pattern for this work. Line the three legs first, then set the dog down, point him at the middle leg, and throw a mark far to your right (if your dog heels on the left). When the dog scoots over to watch the bumper fall, tell him "no!" and take a step toward the pile of bumpers down the middle leg. By throwing the mark to the right, you are positioned between the bumper and the dog. By stepping toward the bumper pile across the pond, you are actually pushing him in that direction. When you get him locked up on the pile of white bumpers, send him. Then, upon his return, have him pick up the mark. Cotton said to make sure the pup is going hard on his pattern work before you start diversions.

"I'd be lining him a lot and I'd be lining him on sight blinds," Cotton said. "Give him so much confidence that he'd almost break on the line gettin' away from me. Then you can start off throwing a diversion, saying 'no!' and lining him. Of course, you have to have the bumpers where he can see them. Then you can start bringing your diversion in closer and closer to that line to the bumper pile. That way, then you can go to two of them.

"After you've got him where you can say 'no!' and line him off in another direction, then throw two bumpers. That's getting pretty hard. Then, if you have to, take two or three steps forward, toward your bumper pile, to get his mind off of these two. Then: 'dead bird...dead bird...back!'"

Cotton said you ought to be able to line an older dog to any bird or bumper you desire. "Unless it's a long bird and he's got to go by a shot bird or something," Cotton said.

This could be especially beneficial in a hunting situation where you see a cripple start to work his way into the brush along the shoreline on the opposite side of the cove and the dog is locked up on the bird your hunting companion has just dropped stone dead 20 yards from the boat. With this kind of diversion training under the dog's belt, you should be able to handle him to that crippled bird without too much of a fight.

When it comes to working on lines and when water is involved, Cotton said, you're going to have to deal with a few problems.

"Always give him those singles first," Cotton said. "And when you line him through there on a sight blind and he cheats, I'd go out there and spank him a little bit. Because a dog will create a habit. If you don't correct it, he'll do it every time. Blow him down with the whistle when he starts to cheat, go out there and whip him a little bit. But not too hard! Then, if you have to, put a rope on him and put him in the water. You're talking about an older dog now, one who knows where he's supposed to be, especially when he's already been over there once and done it the right way. Don't whip a young dog in this situation; work him back up near the water's edge and gradually drop farther back with him."

Cotton said, though, that you won't be able to avoid a few rough sessions.

"During the period of his lifetime and his training," he said, "you're going to have some sessions with him and you're going to have to put a rope on him and a chain (collar), and you're gonna have to make him do what you want him to do."

For example, Cotton discussed a hunting situation which occurred one January several years ago. There were three hunters in the party and one female Labrador retriever. The day was gray, with temperatures in the twenties and a brisk wind blowing in from the north. Lake Pomme de Terre in Missouri's southern waterfowl hunting zone was steadily freezing up. By the time the hunting party motored out of the boat slip near the dam, the coves were cut off with ice. But the wind was keeping the big water open, so the hunters set up off a flooded fencerow and waited for the sun to rise.

Just after sunup, a stray Canada goose fell for their set. On command, the dog hit the icy water like it was an August day in the Ozarks. She fought the chunks of ice that had been drifting through the decoys since first light, and finally made it back to the boat. She sat there, shivering, encased in an icy sheath for the rest of the day. The dog, who bore the scars of four hunting seasons chasing doves, ducks, and pheasants, watched the sky intently.

Finally, about 3 p.m., a group of mallards decided to work. They circled. And circled. And circled again. Finally, as they started to drift higher, obviously ready to head down the lake, one dropped just a little too low and wound up taking a little steel shot in one wing. He hit the water alive about 60 yards out. A quick shot on the water appeared to put him down, and the handler sent the Lab.

In she went, but about halfway out, the duck looked up, saw her coming, and headed for the middle of the lake. The dog couldn't see the duck through the chop. The handler blew his whistle and gave her one cast, but realized that the duck already had too big a head start. He called her back, and the men untied the boat and went after the big greenhead.

When they motored into range, another kill shot left the duck belly-up on the water. The handler sent the dog again, but this time the shivering dog would not go.

The hunter took a deep breath and put the dog back inside the boat. The dog, he said, had never refused to go before. "She's just too cold," he said. The dog sat in the bottom of the boat, wagging her tail, looking up at him.

So, Cotton, how should this have been handled?

"You have to make her go." Cotton said. "I mean she isn't going to be any colder than she already is, right? Just slide her into the water off the bow of the boat. If she gets in the water but till won't go for the duck, you're going to have to use the whip – 'back! back!' You've got to make her get it. The dog has been force broke, right? I would have got on up there with her and shot that duck. Then I would have whipped her and made her get it. Or else I would have put a rope on her and I would have moved that boat around with her in the water swimming until I put her nose right up on that bird and I would have made her fetch.

"It's awful rough on those dogs when it's windy and if they can't get up against a little windbreak or something, sitting out there in the open. Shoot, though, I've had them sit out there on those muskrat houses and they look like a snowball, like pack ice. There just ain't many animals tougher than a retriever."

At this point, your training should be split between training on land and water; for every two days you do land work, do at least three days of water work.

Why the off-balance ratio? Because the water is more difficult to teach and takes so much more time than the land work. On a land double, you can probably work 10 dogs in the time it would take you to work three dogs on a water double.

Although not mandatory, it will greatly simplify your training sessions to have the dog at a high level of proficiency in his lining and handling on the three-legged land pattern before you start handling him in the water.

But, whatever you do, don't bore the dog with these drills. Don't spend every training session for three weeks trying to get the dog to do the channel blind correctly. Work on land marks, water marks, create a few easy sight blinds, repeat old blinds, shoot a few pigeons for him whenever you can. Mix it up, keep it interesting for both of you.

Retrievers, at least in their attitudes about work, run the same gamut as people. Some of them are workaholics, and some of them would rather lie in the shade and watch the world slide by.

Your job as a trainer is to understand your dog, to teach him how to be a good retriever, and to keep him motivated.

It was noon.

The temperature and the humidity were both in the 90's. Cotton said it was time to call it a day, to head back to the house for a little lunch and a glass of iced tea.

Actually, it was time for Cotton to hold court.

Chapter Six

THE HUNTING RETRIEVER

Cotton stopped the truck in front of the kennels. His grandbabies, who had been riding in the back with strict orders to stay seated during the rough ride home from the wildlife area, jumped out and headed for the house. They had "hungry" written all over them.

Cotton put Smoky in his kennel and gave every dog fresh water. Friends, dog-training friends, members of the Missouri River Retriever Club, milled about the backyard.

Jerel Scott was seated at the picnic table. Don Howser, an electrical contractor from nearby Jefferson City, tended to the grill where a heap of ribs was slowly turning brown. Randy Case, a lawn and garden equipment salesman from Holts Summit, sat beside Jerel. The back door opened and Randy's wife, Susan, stepped out with a bowl of potato salad. She was waving at Cotton and smiling. Don's wife Allene followed her with the baked beans. A birthday cake held a prominent spot on the picnic table.

April 3. It was Cotton's birthday.

"Oh, my God," he said. "You all shouldn't have done this."

He took his seat front and center, and someone pushed a birthday present his way. Inside the box was a dozen new bumpers – the big, white ones.

"Oh man," he said. "I better get my initials on these quick before they start showing up in Howser's truck."

This, a standing joke of Cotton's, generated a bit of good-natured razzing which evolved, as just about any type of conversation did in this group, into a hunting story about a dog that was out of control in the dove field, running from hunter to hunter after shot birds – but making sure to stay well away from his owner's part of the field.

This story was like the banging of a gavel, calling Cotton's Court to order.

"You've got to go ahead and concentrate on your dog work when you're hunting," Cotton said, "the same as you would if you were out training him. You ought to explain to 'em (other hunters in the party), 'Now boys, I gotta do this, cause if I don't, I won't be able to do anything with that dog.' And tell 'em your situation."

For the sake of example, Cotton dropped the name of King Buck.

"Shoot, I worked that King Buck's butt plumb over down there (Stuttgart, Arkansas) on a duck hunt. That old duck was fallin' and boy just about the time he hit that water, Ol' Buck hit that water. I called that little booger back and I tore him completely up. And then I had him down there chasin' those running ducks in that shallow water and not stoppin' (on the whistle) and dang right, I worked him over. They had to mind me. I used to be pretty strict and I used to could really run. For fifty yards, maybe seventy-five, I could fly. Now I can't hardly get up and move at all. I'm not as strict as I used to be."

Randy said he had seen some strange reactions to certain situations, especially out of first-time hunting dogs. He told of a dog who could not be coaxed into a boat regardless of what the owner did.

Cotton said if the dog knew the "load" or "kennel" command, he

Don't let a dog "pull your leg," Cotton said. A healthy dog should be able to jump into the bed of a truck to "kennel." Sometimes you have to show him the way with a lead and then reinforce the lesson with a little switching. (Michael McIntosh Photo)

should have gotten into the boat. He explained though, that in certain situations, such as jumping into a truck bed or onto an unstable foundation, like a boat, that the dog might have to be forced. Cotton told of a young dog he had been training that would not jump into a crate on the back of his truck.

"So one day after little D.J. had watched me pick him up and put him in his crate, he said, 'Grandpa, he's pulling your leg.' By God, I thought, he's right. So I had D.J. get up in the truck and we ran a rope through the grate in the back of the crate, out the front, and clipped it onto the dog's collar. I sat him on the bed of that truck and told him to kennel and had D.J. tug on the rope. And he went in. Then I called him out and we did it again and this time along with the tug on the rope, I switched him a little bit and he – zoom! Into that crate he went. So then I sat him on the ground, told him to kennel, and D.J. pulled on that rope and I switched that little booger and up in that crate he went. Now I mean that pup hits that kennel. If you have problems with boats, you could do the same thing. Although most of the time, after a dog understands what happens when he gets in that boat, the shootin' and all, you can't hardly keep him out of it."

Although Cotton is looked upon by today's retriever crowd as a "conventional" trainer, that is, a trainer that does not use an electronic collar, some of his methods might still be perceived as less than conventional.

For example, although retrievers in England are still used to retrieve hares, most hunters in North America prefer that their dogs stick solely to feathers. Cotton developed a drill to break a dog of chasing fur.

"I'd set a dog here, here, here, and here," he said, pointing to the ground in a circle around him. "Now put the rabbit in – a big ol' Belgian hare. And I'd stand here with a bullwhip. Make 'em all sit there, see, they're not supposed to chase fur."

"Why isn't the rabbit going away?" Allene asked.

"He can't," Cotton said. "He just hops around the circle – he's not going to go out and run up through those dogs. He'll run here, then hop over there. I mean, I'm breaking those dogs from chasing and running rabbits or picking up a rabbit. They got to leave that rabbit alone.

"Now if I've got a dog in this group that was too tough for me to handle with all those dogs, what I'd do then, I'd take that dog and put him in the kennel. Then I'd get in that kennel with him, me and Mr. Rabbit and that dog in that kennel. And then, when that dog went after that rabbit, then I got Mr. Dog. Then I'd put that rabbit down again and make him hop all around. By the time I finished, that dog didn't even want to look at that rabbit."

The Wagon Wheel Lining Drill: This is a drill that teaches the dog to go where you point him. In the beginning, you may want to simplify the drill somewhat by picking up only those bumpers at 3 o'clock, 12 o'clock, 9 o'clock, and 6 o'clock. Move the dog around in the center of the circle with the same movements you taught him in the Clock Drill during obedience training. Take your time and try to get the dog to "lock up" on the correct bumper before you send him. Eventually, after you and the dog have refined your movements in the center of the circle, you will want to pick up all the bumpers, "fine lining" him from one bumper to the next. (Michael McIntosh Photo)

Cotton said this fur-breaking drill also gave birth to another drill he used successfully to teach more precise lining – the **Wagon Wheel Drill**:

"Sittin' those dogs in a circle with me in the middle," Cotton said. "That's when it come to me – I'll just make lines, run those dogs down these lines."

To do this drill properly, picture yourself and your dog standing at the center of a clock face. Throw bumpers at 12, 3, 6, and 9. Then throw bumpers deeper between those that are down. You can start the drill using all white bumpers. Use the Clock Drill you taught the dog in his original obedience training to establish the proper lines to the various bumpers.

Since the dog can see these bumpers, you should be able to coax the dog into lining up on the bumper of your choice every time. Make him move with you. Pat your leg and make him heel. Be patient and encourage the dog to move with you from line to line. This is a good point to work on your handling skills as well. It is your job to make sure the dog and you are both lined up on the same bumper. Just to check yourself, have someone stand behind you and make sure you're giving the dog the proper line. This drill, when perfected, will give the dog confidence in your positioning and lining. Later, you can replace the deep ring of bumpers with orange bumpers, which are much more difficult for the dog to see than white bumpers, and make the dog line between the two white bumpers for an orange bumper.

Another training technique that you won't find used by a lot of other trainers – at least retriever trainers – is Cotton's method of aerobic conditioning.

"I used to swim my dogs behind a boat," Cotton told the group. "I would swim them across, like a lake, let 'em get their feet on the ground, if they wanted to, lift their legs or something. Leave them there for a minute or two, then I'd start rowing back the other way and give them that old recall whistle and some of 'em would come off leaping in there, you know. Then I'd take them up and down a channel, back up to the bank, and let them rest and then go again.

"These dogs out here (Cotton points at the kennel), what I've been doing, I drive way back on the farm and I jog 'em. I jog 'em everyday, twice a day. If I don't train them, I'll do it three times a day. You got to watch joggin' a dog. Don't do it more than about ten miles an hour.

"You got to have a dog in good condition for the hunting season. One thing, you can look at that coat, and another thing, look at those muscles. You get an old dog with an old dead coat and that old dead hair, and that dog hasn't had much work. If you take a dog out and work him, he's going to rub a lot of that hair off of him, dryin' off and stuff like that. If you look at those muscles on a dog, in the legs and stuff, heck, you'll see those muscles.

"You can't keep them at top condition all the time, though, there's no way you can do it (similar to conditioning an athlete). Right at the peak. You can get a dog right at the peak, but then you get him over it and you got to let back on him a little bit, and then bring him back."

This discussion evolved into proper diet and care for the dog on the road, for example, on an extended hunting trip.

"I would generally air about three times a day. In the morning, early, when I first got up, I'd air them real good. Then always around one or two o'clock, then I'd feed and I'd air 'em again good in the evening," Cotton said. "Sometimes four times a day. If it was where I had a decent place, and knew the area well, I'd let 'em out again before I went to bed."

Cotton, who traveled extensively both for hunting and field trials, often hit the road with a truckload of dogs. "You can't just let six or seven dogs out someplace where you don't know the area," he added.

"As for feeding, I took care of my dogs very well. I always had them on a good high-protein meal, and then I'd always give them meat – to each one of them. When they was hard-workin' dogs. Cold weather, if I was workin' dogs for a field trial, they would be gettin' about a quarter of a pound of meat.

"Way back, when meat was cheap, when you could get three pounds of hamburger for a quarter, I'd feed 'em hamburger. You could do that. Raw. But when we first started our kennel up there (Nilo) and we went through this here diseases on dogs and stuff (disease research), we used to feed horse meat and we had big cookers, we cooked the horse meat every day in a big container. But horse meat makes their urine have a little too much sugar in it and so beef is better.

"And then, in the winter, those dogs out there will get at least a tablespoon full of oil over their food. Cooking oil. It gives them a little shine and keeps their coats from drying out and it'll make that water get off of 'em a little better. I'll give them oil up until the water starts gettin' warm. I used to give them cod liver oil years ago. I'd give 'em about five or six drops of cod liver oil in their food. One time I gave 'em a little too much and they started smelling fishy. You would of thought I had a damn fish beside me instead of a Labrador. I'll tell you one thing, though, that water would roll right off of them like water off a duck's back.

"Now where you get bad stools a lot of time is overfeeding them. And I don't like to feed anything dry. In the evening, it's all right, you can feed it dry, because then they'll drink enough water that the digestive system will absorb that. But if you was to feed a dog of a morning, now, and go out and work him, the food wouldn't get a chance to digest in his system and it'll make him drink a little more water and he might get a little bloated which could give him diarrhea. If I was going to run 'em, I would soak my feed. They won't drink near as much if you soak that food."

Along with keeping dogs at their peak physical condition, Cotton added that they need to be kept at a high mental level as well. One way to accomplish this is the use of "runners."

Cotton said this is especially effective if the dog tires of hunting his marks and begins to make a habit of "popping."

"Lethargy," Cotton said. "That word covers a lot of things. You need to build 'em up on a lot of birds, game, running birds. It's probably overwork that causes it – the dog's gotten bored. I'm still a great believer in runners, teaching a dog to take a runner – I still think it puts more class and style into 'em."

Cotton said a live duck works well for this drill. Simply shackle or clip the bird's wings. Have an assistant throw the bird high and far so the bird will sail. Add a couple of shots with the blank pistol or shotgun, then send the dog. The duck will walk around, laying down fresh scent. This should get the dog's attention. When the dog finds the bird, the duck will probably try to make an escape, giving the dog a merry chase.

Cotton added that shooting "flyers" also can give a dog an attitude adjustment. The flyer can be a live domestic duck or a live pigeon and the bird simply takes the place of a bumper at one of your gun stations when you are training on marks. Generally, it takes two people to throw and shoot flyer "marks." The flyer will be easiest for the dog if it is shot as the last bird down in a situation involving multiple marks.

Flyers also teach a dog about scent. If your training group includes six or seven dogs, that means six or seven flyer falls. Usually these falls are scattered across a wide vicinity. The dog eventually understands that he must persist in his hunt, piercing through all the fresh scent to find the bird. Flyers are good training for gun dogs, Cotton said, but the flyer gunners need to exercise gun safety the same way they would on a real hunt. And the training situation should not be set up in such a way that the flyer gunners are shooting toward another marking station. This appears to be obvious, but if your gunners have to rush a shot at a bird swinging hard toward another gun station, there could be an accident – especially when the gunners have accounting on their minds and they are determined not to let an $8 domestic mallard escape.

The shot birds can be used at other marking stations too, a good break from the dog's normal routine of bumpers. This, Cotton said, should get a dog fired up about retrieving and, at the same time, give him a lesson in using his nose.

But too many runners or flyers, like too much of a good thing, could create a new problem.

"Now take your little spaniels," Cotton said. "They're a little dog, you know, and they got a very small mouth. Now they'll get them big old live pheasants and they'll bring 'em on in alive. Now of course after a lot of this, after he gets five years old or so, he starts comin' on down with that bird. Don't bet no money he won't kill a bird."

"Why do they do it when they're older and not younger?" Jerel asked.

"Well, they get exposed to so many live roosters and claws on them and stuff like that and that fightin' in their mouth," Cotton said. "They just finally give up. They say, 'We'll stop all that business.'"

Susan, sitting by the birthday cake, nibbling at the icing, piped up: "I've heard that once a dog kills a bird that you'll probably have problems with it from then on."

"Well, that's possible," Cotton said, never one to give 100 percent assurance when it comes to matters of the canine. "But I wouldn't say definitely, all of the time. I used to have a golden. He never killed a duck in his life. But I guarantee you he'd kill a pheasant. Every pheasant he got a hold of, he'd kill. But never, wouldn't even ruffle a feather on a duck. You could throw a hundred ducks for him to retrieve and he'd never mess with one of them. But a pheasant – he hated 'em!

"I've fixed up a lot of things to try to cure it. I have a harness with a lot of tacks driven through it. You can put it around the ducks, under their wings. I make my own. The tacks are about this long (he holds up his thumb and forefinger spread about 3/8"), and when they grab that and come down, they hit those tacks. Sometimes that will work effectively on a dog.

"But, a truly hardmouthed dog, you're going to have to worry about him all the time. Always. You can't say that you can break one. I mean, I never could and I think I could train a dog just as good as anybody could. And I never could get one that I didn't have to worry about at a field trial or hunting, whether he was going to kill a bird on me."

This spawned a question about another hard-to-fix problem – gunshyness.

Cotton said the best cure is buying another dog, but he added, "A lot of people used to break gunshyness through feeding. They'd put the dog's feed down in the kennel and shoot a shotgun and if that dog ran and didn't eat, they said, 'Hell with you brother,' and took the food bowl. Then they'd go back the next day, *bang!* And if he runs back in the house, they'd take the food bowl. This might go on for several days but pretty soon that dog will start eating during the shooting and then you got him."

There was a pause in the conversation. The ducks made contented noises in Cotton's pen out by the kennels. A gentle breeze was blowing. Cotton looked down into his plate of food and, as if the bare rib bones spoke to him, he shook his head and said, "Andy Devine."

Puzzled looks, then a communal cupping of the ear. Everyone knew when Cotton was leading up to a story.

"He used to have some Labradors and he ran the field trials. Well, he was down there in California and he was huntin' ducks. Old Andy used to tell this story. You know he had that real high-pitched, kind of whiney voice. Well, he said, 'Cotton, I was walking along this here irrigation ditch and, man, I dropped a sprig over there.' I forget what dog it was. But anyway, Andy said, 'He hit that water and he went over there. He got that duck and he came back over there and standing up on that bank, he looked at me. I said, 'Come on boy,' and I blew that whistle and he looked at me again. What do you think he did, Cotton?' I said, 'I don't know, what'd he do, Andy?' He said, 'He laid that duck down and he looked at me again. 'Come on boy, fetch him up! Heel!' And man he started pickin' them feathers off that duck and spittin' just like watermelon seeds and he started eatin' that duck.' He said, 'Cotton, you know I'm big and that ditch wasn't very wide, and I thought I could run and jump it. So I run and jumped and I fell in right about here and I had my gun.' He said, 'That sonofagun, he made a mistake, though.' He said, 'He come down there to see what happened. And when he did I took that gun and I hit that so-and-so.

The late Andy Devine, an actor who starred in movies and television at the time, was an active field trial competitor as well as a shooter for the national stakes. He poses during the 1952 National Championship Stake at Weldon Springs, Missouri, with 1951 NFC Ready Always of Marianhill, owned by Mahlon B. Wallace Jr. of St. Louis.

And I broke my gunstock. And it was my Parker!' And you know how his voice was whiney. 'But I broke that damn dog from eatin' ducks.'"

The coals in the grill popped and sizzled. Cotton, too, was getting warmed up. Cotton's wife, Mayrene, who had joined the party midway through the story, reminded him of a trip to England. Cotton said he was invited on a driven pheasant shoot while they were there but he had not been able to attend.

"But I've seen 'em. People over there on Long Island used to have this big place. I've been on several of 'em, on drive shoots with a dog; when I was over in England we were invited on some of those shoots but we never did go. It's very expensive. Course if you're not invited as a guest, you can't go anyway.

"But on Long Island, they were doing exactly the same. They'd have beaters comin' in on these birds, see, and you'd better not have a noisy dog on the (shooting) line because if you did you took him out right away. No noise at all. He was supposed to be very calm and quiet, see, cause they're drivin' them birds. And if the dog is barkin' here, them birds are going to fly the other way. A man named...what was his name, now? Anyway, he was the old man that ran this place for Marshall Field. So anyway, the old man says, 'Cotton would you like to bring a couple of dogs on the shoot?' Which was quite an honor. Well, I had Tar of Arden and Old Rip with me. Shoot, we put on a show for 'em."

Cotton added that he taught all of his retrievers to work like spaniels in those days, which means they were taught to quarter and flush upland birds such as pheasants and quail. He said most birdy dogs will quarter naturally, given enough opportunity. But, with just a little drilling on pigeons, you can have them quartering like an oldtimer in no time.

"Put some pigeons out there (in the cover). Shake 'em about five or six times (to dizzy them, to make them stay put), then put some stakes down to indicate a course. This gives you some guidelines. Tell that dog to 'hi on' or whatever you use to let him loose and start walking down your course. Now the dog is whistle broke when you're teaching this, so if he gets over too far or too deep, toot! toot! (call him in). Plant the birds far enough apart that when they get shot, the dog has plenty of room to go out there and mark that fall and pick it up without flushing another bird."

Cotton said all the retrievers at Nilo from Tar of Arden to the greatest Nilo dog of all, King Buck, worked both in field trials and as hunting dogs. Cotton talked of the 12,000-acre Nilo Plantation in Georgia with as much reverence as was in the man. He talked of beautiful days afield, of mounted bird dog handlers, and of mule-drawn gunning wagons. Up top, alongside the driver, would sit Cotton's pride and joy, his retrievers.

"We started in '55," Cotton said. "No one ever had better wagon dogs than we had. We had the cream of the crop. Hell, King Buck's been on that wagon. Yes sir. And that Ace of Spades, field trial champion Ace of Spades, has been on that wagon. All them big champions, they been up on that wagon. Mr. Olin believed in working those dogs. He said, 'You're such a great dog trainer, let's see what you can do down here, now.' Yessir.

"One day, we were going along and Mr. Olin dropped one out into a pond about 150 yards. Hell, he hit him in the head and that bird elevated and went a waaaaaaaay out and finally he turned it loose and down he went. I was up on the horse and he said, 'Pershall,' he said, 'Now you got such a national champion up there, you think he can get that bird?' I said, 'Mr. Olin, he can get a bird anywhere you put him.'

140

So I took the dog off, I put my hand down, and I lined him up and I said, 'Buck...back!' He went out there and just hit it right on top of the head.

"Ace of Spades was the same way. In a great big swamp, where that swamp grass was about that high, just where you could see his tail up there. And I had a bird marked – I used to could mark; I could mark a bird in a spot the size of this table, anywhere you could put it. Anyway, I took that little black dog out there, that Ace of Spades, and boy, boy, boy...back! peep, over! And *whoom*, on that bird and here he come and away we went!

"I used all my field trial dogs to pick up birds on the shoots over at Nilo. On ducks and stuff. Oh yeah. I read an article in one of them books in there (he jerked his thumb in the direction of the house) about somebody talking about field trial dogs. He says if it wasn't for the field trial dogs, we wouldn't have as good a shooting dog as we

Cotton talks fondly of John Olin (left), more like a son talking about his father than an employee talking about his boss. They spent countless days afield together, shooting ducks and quail and watching the dogs run at field trials. They posed for the camera here at the 1952 National Championship Stake. Roy Gonia, another great retriever trainer of the era, flanks Cotton on the right.

have now. He said they're higher class, they're better-trained dogs, and it's done a lot for shooting dog people to make them have better, well-trained shooting dogs. What was that old slogan, retrievers were for conservation? How did that wording go? 'More dogs and better dogs in the interest of conservation.' I believe that was the slogan. I think it's right. One place, in some state it was, several years back, they allowed one extra duck if you had a retriever with you. I can't remember now what state it was, whether it was Jersey or where, but I think that's right!"

Cotton talked about the old days afield with John Olin as if the master of Olin Industries were sitting at the picnic table, licking barbecue sauce off his fingers, ready at the drop of a hat to load a couple of good dogs and head to Arkansas for a duck shoot.

"We was down at Stuttgart," Cotton began, "and the director of Winchester Arms was with us. So he had this old Labrador bitch he called Molly. And I had this big string of mine down there, too. I mean a rough string! I had Buck and (Freehaven) Muscles and all of 'em. So he was up there and he was telling this story. This was way back. So anyway, Mr. Olin, he was sitting there and this old boy says, 'Now old Molly,' he says, 'I shot this bird here, it was awful high, it was terrible high and it came right down and hit the ice and went through the ice. I sent Molly to get that bird and Molly went out there to where that duck went down in that hole and she went down in that hole and I couldn't see Molly or nothin'. Then about a hundred yards, there's open water and here comes Molly. Out she came with that duck.'

"Well then he tried to work her on a little ditch there, just in front of the blind, trying to get her to go across there and get something, and she wouldn't even go. Mr. Olin says, 'I've listened to enough of that damn talk.' he says, 'Go put that ol' coon dog up and, Cotton, show these people some good dogs, will you.' Ha!"

Back in those days, Olin would rent a whole floor at the Riceland Hotel in Stuttgart, Mayrene said.

"They'd wake you up and tell you the temperature," Cotton said. "Then you'd go down and have your breakfast and come back up to your room and brush your teeth, put your boots on, and get down in the lobby. The car would be waiting there where it could take you out to the clubhouse. The guides would be there and they'd put you in a boat and take you to the blinds. I'd have my dogs up in them big boats, just sittin' up there.

"There were always a few celebrities around. Robert Taylor, now he was a good-lookin' boy (to which Mayrene heartily agreed!). He was a pretty good shooter, too. He was all man. He wasn't like a sissy boy. I'll tell you somebody else that was all man, that Dale Robertson. He was tall, about six-foot-two. He doesn't look it in his pictures. But, God Almighty, could he ride a horse. He could sing pretty good, you know. We had (James) Arness, Taylor, all those boys. Old Andy (Devine) was a good shot too."

The talk of old friends and acquaintances eventually turned to Paul Bakewell III, a man that started a young, towheaded boy from Arkansas in the retriever business more than 50 years ago. One story in particular stood out.

"There was a terrible storm," Cotton said, leaning back against the picnic table, looking off into the distance. "Bakewell, he went up there during that Armistice Day (1940) when they had that terrible storm. You know, when people lost their lives. He had old Rip and Tar with him that day. And he got down in one of them kind of sand holes, you know, along with river and he almost drowned. He called them dogs over to him where he could kind of get ahold of them and they pulled and crawled around and got out of that quicksand. He said, 'Cotton, they saved my life.' Old Rip, he weighed around a hundred pounds.

"Bakewell – he lived a hundred lives. He used to be such a strict Catholic, that on their collars – he used to have just a choke chain – on their collars they wore a little St. Christopher Cross. He even had that station wagon blessed when I drove it. I had one in the glove box, one of those Crosses. I really did. Yeah, those dogs, yeah, they had one on their necks, damn right. They used to wear them in the field trials until they (sanctioning body) made 'em stop wearing chains."

It was turning into one of those idyllic spring afternoons, Even the ancient oak tree that shaded Cotton's kennel seemed to stretch and yawn. There were lulls in the chatter, moments of introspection.

But then the conversation turned to competition, to the field trial. An element of dog training that was as close to Cotton's core as black dogs named Buck. The field trial contingent was off to the races.

JOHN MERRILL OLIN
EAST ALTON, ILLINOIS

December 24, 1965

Dear Nash:

I appreciated the note written on your Christmas
card and was delighted to see a Model 21 and a beautiful
Labrador comprising the card. I think the Labrador is one
of our breeding and, of course, the gun is a Winchester
Model 21.

Cotton was fortunate in winning the National
Championship. It had been twelve years since his last
win with KING BUCK. He had three of the nine dogs called
back for the tenth series which is really an outstanding
performance. Also, he won the Derby Championship for this
year so it has truly been a red-letter year for him and for
me.

With every good wish to Irma and you for a
wonderful holiday season,

Sincerely,

John

Mr. Nash Buckingham
198 South McLean Boulevard
Memphis, Tennessee

A letter from one outdoor giant to another about a third – John Olin writes to
Nash Buckingham of Cotton's 1965 success. (Letter courtesy Dr. Dyrk Halstead and
Robert Urich)

Chapter Seven

THE FIELD
TRIAL RETRIEVER:
COTTON'S WAY

The two men at the picnic table, Jerel and Randy, tossed field trialing "what if's..." back and forth and Howser tried to point out the reasonable conclusions or what a judge would do with a dog's given behavior. His pointer was a rib bone that dripped barbecue sauce on the sidewalk where he stood.

In the usual Midwestern "get together," after a hearty meal, the women retire to the kitchen to discuss matters feminine and the men head for the den or the living room to catch the latest sports scores.

But, this was not a usual group. These were field trialers where women wield their own whipping sticks and where men listen when the women talk.

The debate focused on a set of marks, a triple, at a past field trial. The working dog had to be handled on the last bird for which he was sent. The debate dealt with the moment of truth: When do you start to handle? Could the dog have found the bird without the handler's help?

Cotton, listening, finally had heard enough.

"When you're running a dog and they (the judges) put that great big 'H' on you, that means 'handle,' and you're hurt. And if you get two of them, you're o-u-t. And, on top of that, a lot of these dogs will pop if you overhandle on marks. After they've had a pretty hard hunt, they'll come up with that nose in the air and sit down and look back at you like a Scotch prince out there. That's what I call poppin'. When a dog pops on a mark, that's a cardinal sin, terrible. I haven't got no use to look at him anymore. He's give up his hunt.

"I had a bad reputation of not blowing whistles on marks. I would just hardly ever handle on a mark. Then when I started judgin', a lot of those boys thought I liked that kind of work. And then I would eliminate 'em from a trial for lettin' their dogs hunt great big. You gotta know your judges."

It was generally agreed upon that, in today's field trial, a handle in the first series of marks or the first marking test of an open all-age stake means elimination – unless a large percentage of the entries are handled.

Cotton said he has seen many changes in the field trial game over the past 50 years.

"They've changed a lot," he said, leaning back in his chair, hands clasped behind his head. "Back then (the 40's and 50's), we had a lot of walk-ups and a lot more marks. They were closer birds, but tough birds.

"I don't think the dogs are any better. I think they (the judges) stress too much now on lining. As a judge, I like to go about sixty-forty – about sixty percent marking and about forty percent on blinds. That goes for a national (championship stake) too. I'd like to have six series marking and say maybe four series blinds.

"I think the dogs way back years ago, if they were trained like these dogs are, could do as well as these dogs, maybe do better. We used to have better game-finders. We worked them on game a lot more than they do now. A lot of these dogs (today) don't see a bird until they come to a field trial.

"Put it this way, I don't think dogs nowadays could beat our dogs back years ago in the tests that we had, and I don't think our dogs back years ago would beat these dogs today in a field trial. Especially on blinds.

"We just didn't stress that line too much. If he (the dog) went down there (along the bank) fifteen or twenty feet, it was 'toot' and put him in there (with a cast). But now, (in training) they call him back (trying to get a better line) and hone him so much that they make a cow out of him, you know, a pig. What the hell is the difference? That fifteen or twenty feet, or that style?"

There was more than a little irony in Cotton's conversation. After all, in his day, his dogs were the best lining dogs of all.

But judging was still the focus of conversation. Cotton said that after his retirement as a professional in 1975, he reclaimed his amateur status and became a popular field trial judge. For awhile.

Unlike most of Cotton's memories, these weren't particularly fond.

"Everybody thought I was a great judge there for a long time. But then, like when I'd have someone shoot a gun beside his dog, well, the electric collar people put the big kick in to stop that – from using a gun on the line. They figured if a trainer had a gun in his hand, his dog wasn't going to break. Or he'd handle better, see, because they didn't have the (electronic) collar on the dog's neck.

"The collar people changed that. They eliminated that. Then they figured that my birds were too close, toward the end. They thought they were too short and they didn't know how to train for them, whatever that means.

"I haven't quit judgin'. I just haven't been asked. I haven't been asked for a couple of years, maybe three years."

The first question that comes to mind is why would the "collar people" want to abolish the use of a shotgun next to the working dog? The feeling was that a shotgun at the line gave the conventional trainer an unfair advantage. The shotgun would intimidate the conventionally trained dog, because the shotgun was a key training aid for that particular style of trainer. For example, if, during a training session, a dog slipped a whistle or two, the conventional trainer peppered the dog with No. 9 shot in an effort to enforce the whistle command. A smart retriever, maybe even a dumb one, learns pretty quickly that when there's a shotgun handy, he'd better pay attention to his handler.

Cotton admitted, though, that the major changes, the changes that affected him directly, occurred at Nilo.

"We changed at Nilo," Cotton said. "We started our shooting patrol business there then. It got so big that we never had time to really concentrate on winning the national like we did before, when we had Buck. And we were lucky on Martens Little Smoky (the 1965 National Champion).

"I took him back East. I was back there for about three or four trials. I had to go by myself. I didn't even have anybody to take along to take the edge off of a dog.

"And at the area (Nilo), where I could work, there was hunters in there – on all the courses! I could be by myself and go out and do a blind, but I'd have to get off the course or go some place else. You know, that's exactly what cut us down or we'd had a couple of more (national champions). It was our time element. We didn't have the time to train and run the dogs. We were on those shootin' patrols too much. Shooting preserve work. I'd run a duck shoot in the mornings and go out by myself in the afternoon and my boys would be out with them (hunters) in the pheasant field. I think Nilo's shooting preserve

In the early days of retriever field trials, the dogs often worked out of the three-sided, simulated duck blinds pictured here. The dog was sent through the hole in the front panel to make his retrieves. Keith's Black Magic comes around behind the blind to deliver a bird to Cotton during the Open All Age stake at the Long Island Retriever Club trial held near Huntington, New York in October of 1946.

got too big for us to make more national champions. I think we could have had one or two more if we had more time to spend on our field trial dogs.

"I did used to take them (the trial dogs) down on the duck drives, though. If I had one that was pretty jumpy, I'd take him down and make him a little steady. It was a great place to steady a dog. Those ducks comin' over and they're (hunters) dropping 'em and the ducks are hitting four or five feet from you. There might be a cripple and he'd start floppin' his wings or maybe trying to run, you know that's a good place to work on steadying a dog.

"That's still pretty basic, though, that dog has got to sit there until that man sends him. I don't know if you all ever noticed, but at a field trial, it's a long bird flyer that'll break a dog more than a close one because that dog's thinkin', 'Boy, they're testin' me. I'm not going out there and gettin' that bird.' But get those damn long flyers out there, and it gets him going."

Cotton rolled back into the old days without even taking a breath.

148

"Boy, you had to honor then," he said. "And that dog had to be steady. We used to have 'em thrown right over our heads. Ducks, thrown right over our heads when we were in those little ol' blinds (three-sided plywood contraptions with a hole cut in the front for the dog). And then we had to sit 'em out there on kind of a little stool. I used to call it a pedestal. Sit him out there and you had to go get in that blind. They'd shoot the birds and that dog had to be steady now. Then you sent him from the blind to make the retrieves. Sometimes they had to honor for three birds, too. Sometimes you had three dogs on the line and you had to honor for all three of 'em.

"Let me give you a tip about that: If you've got a breaking dog and after you work him, don't stand right next to him on the honor. He's not as likely to break over there four or five feet from you as he is if you're standing next to him. Just sit your dog down and walk over nonchalant and fold your hands."

Randy, always one to take advantage of an opening and the best what-if man in the group, said, "What if you had one of those three-bird honors and you got a no-bird (a missed bird, or one that falls in a location that is not a fair retrieve)?"

"You still honored," he said. "You stayed there. I was on the line one time and this dog of mine saw seventeen shot pheasants before I ever got to send him. This was back in '38 or '39, I forget which. Up at Averell Harriman's place. But they've changed the rules a lot. They've got away from staunchin' tests.

"Why back at Harriman's estate, they ran them (field trials) like they did in England, like on a drive, you know. That's the way they judged the field trial. They might have eight, nine, ten dogs there on the line. These birds are driven birds and they shoot 'em coming over. Anyway, I was there for one trial and this was a duck drive. They were judgin' markin' on these dogs on this duck drive. It wasn't over water, it was on land. And trees. I had that Tar of Arden bitch with me and I was on the line. They shot this bird and it walked up right under Tar, right here in front of her. That duck came up and sat down there! Her eyeballs – I mean I was here, the dog was here and that duck was right there. And they (the judges) called another dog's number and he come in there and picked that bird up!"

As one, the group howled. Somebody said it sounded like an invitation for a dog fight.

"Years ago a dog had to know how to handle a runner (a crippled bird that ran off after being shot) too," Cotton said. "If a dog had a runner, they'd better know how to work it, and they'd better take it. Then they had to have a nose. Nowadays, there are a lot of dogs that couldn't take a runner. Back then, though, if a dog couldn't take a runner, the judges didn't feel that he had much of a nose or else he wasn't trained on it.

"Oh they used to be rough. Triple walk-ups. Live decoys! But that was before my time. They started licensed field trails back about '35, and I started in the spring of '38.

And a year later, Cotton won the *Field & Stream* Trophy, an honor bestowed on the high-point open dog for the year. The dog was a golden named Rip. Cotton repeated the feat in 1940 and before Rip was through, he collected 63 open points.

"As good a dog as I ever had," Cotton said. "He was a good one, one that would fly and hit that water. But he was a tough little rat! This dog was tough! He had been on the duck shoots, too, up around Havana, Illinois. We (Bakewell and Cotton) started off with goldens, just goldens. Rip was the first golden to win an open stake in the United States."

Shed of Arden and Tar of Arden came along shortly thereafter. Another little dog, Treveilyr Swift, who was an English champion as well as an American Field Champion and a Canadian Field Champion, held a special spot in Cotton's heart.

"I had a running pheasant at a trial once with him," Cotton said. "I

Treveilyr Swift prepares to deliver a duck to his handler Edward Spaulding during the 1953 National Championship Stake near Easton, Maryland. The little field champion, who was suffocated in the cargo hold of an airplane, is immortalized in an oil painting that hangs above Cotton's fireplace.

Marvadel Black Gum, the 1946 Derby Champion and the 1949 National Champion, retrieves a mallard shot during the 1953 National Championship Stake. Cotton once won a derby stake and an open all-age stake at the same trial with this dog. Cotton said the dog made his title (Field Champion) at 18 months of age.

saw that pheasant come up and go down that road and go underneath a car. The judges couldn't see it and they called my number and I sent Swift and boy he worked and worked and he could really take a runner. And, oh, it was hot! Anyway, the judge, he says, 'Cotton, it's awful hot, I think you'd better pick him up.' I said, 'Wait just a minute. This dog is workin' that bird. Now he'll pick that bird up, just give me another couple of minutes and see what he does.' About that time, I saw Swift hit the road and cut right toward the cars. I just rared back and I said, 'He'll be here with that bird in less than a minute and a half.' And, God Almighty, about fifty yards down there, that old bird went up and smack! Swift had him and here he came. I got second with him that day."

But the little dog, immortalized in an oil painting that hangs in Cotton's living room, ran out of luck along the way.

"He suffocated on an airplane going to California," Cotton said, shaking his head. "They packed stuff all around his crate and on top. I think it wound up costing the airplane company $10,000. He was quite a little dog."

Then along came Marvadel Black Gum who was the 1946 National Derby Champion, the 1949 National Open Champion, and the winner of the *Field & Stream* Trophy for that year.

"I won a derby and an open at the same trial with that dog." Cotton said. "He was a field champion at eighteen-months old. At the time, he was the youngest one that had ever been made."

Then, of course, there was King Buck, whose story has been told many times. Cotton also recalls one of Buck's kennelmates, a dog

Cotton receives a duck from FC Black Point Dark Destroyer, owned by Daniel E. Pomeroy of Englewood, New Jersey, during the 1952 National Championship Stake. He said Destroyer almost beat King Buck for the title that year.

that offered the most serious competition to the legendary King Buck in the 1952 national championship stake. The dog's name was Black Point Dark Destroyer, and if the memory of Buck and his expertise in the field trial game and as a gun dog are at the top of Cotton's list, the memory of Dark Destroyer is somewhat farther down.

"He damn near won that '52 national," Cotton told the group. "But he was the filthiest dog. He'd mess in his crate and I'd have to go out there and wash his crate out in the morning. Then I'd throw dummies in the lake to wash the stuff off of him! I told the owner, I says, 'Take him. I can't do anything with him. Put him with any other trainer you want.'

"Then he started winning. I got a second with him. I told the owner and the owner wanted me to keep running him. I said, 'Now, you can let anybody else run him that you want to.' I was still trying to get rid of him, see. Next week, the son-of-a-gun won. And boy, he started gettin' hot and I was winning or placing with him every trial. He was still nasty. Nasty 'til the day he died. And I mean I almost won that '52 national with him, almost beat Buck with him. Anyway, about the fourth or fifth time the dog won, the owner says, 'Pershall, you don't know so much about dogs after all, do you?' I said, 'No...no

Smoky, Cotton's last national champion, returns with a shot pheasant during the 1965 National Championship Stake held at the Bombay Hook National Wildlife Refuge near Smyrna, Delaware.

sir, I guess not.' And I took his check and put it in my pocket."

And then there was Cotton's last national champion, Martens Little Smoky. In 1965, Cotton and Smoky made the pages of *Sports Illustrated.*

The writer, Duncan Barnes, interviewed Cotton and recorded Cotton's achievements to that point in his career:

> "*A husky, 51-year-old Arkansan with sandy hair, Pershall has managed Industrialist-Sportsman John Olin's modern, antiseptic Nilo Kennels in East Alton, Ill., for 14 years and has turned out some 25 champion field trial Labradors. His record in the nationals is unassailable – he has qualified 81 dogs for 21 nationals, won the championship four times (three times with Olin's dogs) and trained two more dogs that went on to win for others.*"

The interview also described those qualities Cotton most enjoyed in a working retriever and, almost in passing, Cotton's attitude about "currently popular electronic devices":

> *"'Smoky had it from the start,' says Pershall. 'He had class, which covers most everything – speed, good nose, eagerness – and he was a very brainy dog. Lots of young fireballs just fold up under serious training, but Smoky was the kind of tough dog that could take correction and still enjoy the game.' Regarded by most field trialers as a 'gentler trainer than most,' Pershall shuns all of the currently popular electronic devices such as shock collars and transistorized radio transmitters."*

In 1965, Cotton Pershall did not like what electronic collars could do to his beloved retrievers; a quarter-century later, Cotton Pershall still didn't like the "shock collar."

"One thing it has created," Cotton said. "One thing I don't like about the collar, is when a dog is out there hunting, like on a mark, and say it's a triple. Say on the third bird or the second bird. Just take any bird. And he makes two or three sashays huntin' out there. You watch him. He gets kind of a frightened spell. He's on his own and that's dangerous to him. He's afraid he's going to get buzzed, and then he loses his natural hunting ability about him. He loses style. He's still moving – but he's afraid he's going to have that juice hit him.

"Where they've really been burnt and ate up with it, is when they start off, like on blinds. The further he goes, the faster he'll get. He knows he's doing right. By the time he gets a hundred and fifty yards out there he's running, but the first fifty or sixty yards, he's a pig."

Cotton describes why he thinks this happens:

"It was at Nilo. I was waiting in the car, watching another pro training a dog with one of those collars. He was running this dog down there and *zzzzzzt!* Then he'd call him back. It was down alongside this road. He'd send him again and *zzzzzt!* I watched about ten minutes, and I was wantin' to get back on to some other people, to see if I could be of any help, you know, take 'em birds or see if they needed shells or anything. So anyway, I decided to talk to this fellow. I said, 'You know,' I says, 'I've been in this dog game a long time and I like to learn. I'd like to know what it is that you're doing.' Well, he says, 'Cotton, you see that shadow down there in the road, from that tree?' and I said, 'Yep.' He says, 'I want him (the dog) to go right at that shadow, right on the edge of that shadow.' 'Well,' I said, 'I'll tell you what. I've been sitting there for about fifteen minutes now, watchin' you, and that shadow has moved about six feet. Now I says, 'That doesn't make sense does it?' Really! He says, 'You know, I didn't think about that.' Man, he was grindin' him up and he'd call him back and that dog would go again. He was a tough baby."

Although Cotton is dead set against using the electronic collar, he does admit that it is an effective training tool – in the right hands. He said the problem is, there are just too many trainers who abuse them. Losing your temper and abusing a dog with a whip or a lead and chain collar during a training session can create problems that are hard to overcome; make the same mistake with an electronic collar, and the problems may be impossible to fix. Cotton, who used a shotgun and shells loaded with birdshot to make long-range corrections, said he used such methods only when necessary.

"I do very little with a shotgun," he said. "When I think it's the time to do it, to get him back in the grove, well, then I'd do it. You can't do it every day, 'cause if you do, you're going to make a pig out of a dog – with a shotgun or an electric collar. I think a person who really knows how to use an electric collar, I don't think there's anything wrong with it. If a person's got the right temperament. But you have some people that get mad, hotheaded, and they say, 'I'll fix you, I'll grind you up!' then *zzzzzzt!*"

Cotton recalled with a grin one of his few experiences with an electronic collar.

"Ol' Billy Wunderlich (a professional trainer) came over there (to Nilo) one day and this old yellow dog I had – he had so much natural ability about him and I used him on a lot of runners, used him on the shoots. But when you hit him with the whistle, you could count about 'one...two...three,' then he'd put it down.

"He wasn't getting it down tight enough, and I figured I'd get in a tight spot someday and lose him, so I thought I'd just try that (electronic collar) on him someday.

"So old Wunderlich came over and I said, 'Bill, let me try that collar on that son-of-a-gun.' He said okay, so I sent that dog out there, man, and I hit him with that whistle 'peep' and then the collar and that son-of-a-gun came at me. I crawled on top of that damn station wagon right quick. And I said, 'No, no, Rusty! No! I didn't do that.' And I said the hell with that thing (the collar). The only way I was going to use that on him was have him tied to a tree. That was before they got it down pretty fine. But I'll tell you, when one of 'em thinks you're going to do it to him, now, he'll get you."

Cotton said he has seen the exact opposite happen, a bolting dog, as a result of too much pressure.

"Wunderlich was back there training at Sweezey's (another professional trainer) in Maryland there, around Chester, so he had this great big old dog, he'd weigh almost a hundred pounds," Cotton said. "Anyway, he bolted on old Bill. And man they hunted for him and they hollered for him. He just took off. They finally walked back up to the truck and there he was. Bill had left his window down in the truck and he'd done messed all up in that truck and walked in it. Just all over that truck.

"They will take off sometimes even with that electric collar. I knew a boy who had this happen. The dog bolted and he couldn't find him so he ran an ad in the paper, 'Send collar home...keep dog.'"

A breeze ruffled the paper napkins on the picnic table. Allene and Jerel carried dishes into Mayrene's kitchen. Susan came out of the door with a fresh stack of plates for the birthday cake. Cotton, smiling, crossed his arms across his chest.

When the table was cleared and the candles lit, an off-key version of Happy Birthday was sung. And when the wisecracking and laughter died down, Jerel asked Cotton about a situation that had occurred at a field trial the weekend before.

"It was the first series, a land triple," Jerel said. "The dog had great work but when he came back with the third bird, he wouldn't give it up. The handler did everything you could do and that dog wouldn't relax his grip. They finally wound up taking him off the line with the bird in his mouth. It was a weird deal, Cotton. You ever see anything like that before?"

"Oh, my God, yes! That Marvadel Black Gum I was telling you about, that I won a derby and an open with at the same trial? He turned out to be one of the worst 'freezers.' But he never did freeze on me. Why? It's hard to say, but in his case I would say it had to be from sloppy work on delivery by the handler, getting the bird from him, or pulling on a cripple."

"Is this something a handler always causes?" Jerel asked.

"I think they help," Cotton said, "And I think a dog's traits – that it's in certain bloodlines, like on Freehaven Muscles. Freehaven Muscles was a freezer. That is he was a little bit reluctant to release. A lot of his gets, or like his grandsons, down the line, those babies do it. He had a tendency to want to stay with that bird a little bit. That's my thinkin', anyway."

Jerel asked if freezing could be fixed by force training.

"It will help some dogs," Cotton said, "and some dogs it won't. You get a dog that's never been force broke properly, then he starts freezin', force breakin' might stop him. Force breakin' could bring it on in some dogs, especially certain ways of force breakin'. If you force break 'em with an electric collar and you get too severe, you might get a dog that, really, will stick on a bird. I mean, you know, he doesn't want to turn it loose because he knows he's supposed to grab it.

"A person being up there nervous (in a field trial situation) could bring it on too. Maybe the bird is still alive and they're nervous and they get a hold of it and try to pull it out before the dog really opens his mouth.

"Most of the time a dog is going to freeze on a bird, he's gonna circle you a time or two before he freezes. In training, use that pinch collar and that rope to get him up to you. I mean smash him into you. And if you get that collar on him and that check cord and if you give him a good lesson, I'll guarantee, he'll try to break that damn leg comin' in there. Then, in a trial situation, you might want to fresh his memory up a little bit on that collar and lead before you go to the line.

"I don't really know why they do it (freeze), though. But you watch at any trial. When a dog goes to freeze on a man, that ol' dog will go around and slink in there like that. And where a lot of 'em (handlers) go wrong, they reach out and grab it (the bird). Then the tug-of-war is on. Make him come up in there and sit! If it looks like he's going to freeze, about the only thing you can do is just put a little authority in that voice – 'heel!'"

Cotton described a last-ditch method that an oldtimer had used to cure a freezer: The dog froze on a bird, the trainer told him to leave it, the dog would not drop, so the trainer told him again, 'leave it,' and swatted the dog across the ears with a blackjack while he held the bird. Cotton said the dog dropped the bird and from then on, during a field trial, if the dog showed the signs of freezing while he was coming in with a bird, all the handler had to do was reach for the bird with his right hand and move his left hand behind the dog's head. The movement was just enough of a threat to make the dog drop the bird in a hurry.

"There was another trainer, I saw him at the St. Louis field trial a long time ago. He had this little dog, I think her name was Counterpoint, I'm not sure. And she was a freezer. And this trainer knew that he was out (of the field trial) anyway and the dog froze on a bird, so he took the bird in his hand and came down on top of her head with his other hand. And the judge turned his head like he was writin' in his book. I think this probably helped break this dog of freezin'."

Cotton pointed out that freezing is a different problem than hardmouth.

"No, a hardmouthed dog is a dog that cracks those bones and chews on those birds," Cotton said. A freezer is not necessarily killing the bird or even damaging the bird; he's just not giving it to the handler. In the modern field trial, Cotton said, hardmouth goes unpunished, and it is not necessarily the fault of the judges.

"There is no way, right now, that you can knock a dog out for hardmouth at a field trial where they're usin' these ducks over and over – unless he just sits out there and eats the dang bird. How are you going to judge a dog on delivery? The duck (he retrieves) might have been thrown fifteen times for fifteen different dogs. There might have been three or four of those dogs that really got a hold on that bird. I've had 'em come back in like that and after the trial, there wasn't even a whole bone left in that bird's body for a dog to crack."

Cotton said before the American Kennel Club banned the use of shackled birds in field trials, a hardmouthed dog was easy to spot.

"I was judgin' in Minnesota," Cotton said. "There were four birds in the water, four shackled birds. This old dog killed all four birds. The dog did beautiful work otherwise.

"Well, I dropped the dog and later I saw the handler comin' my way. I said, 'Now wait a minute. Before you come any farther,' I said, 'I know what you're coming over here for, so don't come over here mad,' cause if you do I'm going to knock your head off.' So he started grinning. 'He killed all four birds,' I said and he said, 'Well, I knew he killed two or 'em but I didn't think you all caught it.' I told him I wasn't blind or deaf. Man, I mean I could hear the bones crackin'."

Cotton said field trial handlers, since the early days of the game, have used subtle forms of intimidation in an effort to get better performances out of their dogs.

"Like this fellow Bakewell, that I used to work for," Cotton said. "We had this dog called Matchmaker. He was a popper. Well Bakewell taught ol' Matchmaker that when he moved his hand like that (a flicking of the wrist) he was supposed to go back. The judges were generally watching the dog and couldn't see the movement, and here he'd go. Ol' Matchmaker would look over his shoulder before he'd pop and Bakewell would flick that wrist and here he'd go.

"And Chuck (Charlie Morgan). He used to be a devil too. He'd sneeze and make that dog sit (while the dog was honoring). You know a dog can hear so well. I used to hiss at 'em and man, them judges wouldn't hear you, but those dogs could.

"A lot of this game is a fad thing too. I used to wear gloves all the time. I wore 'em on account of the sun on my hands and I did wear white gloves. I wore the gloves for that, and I also used 'em for correction. You know, you can get a pair of gloves and swat a dog with those gloves to make him sit in training and sometimes, if the dog was acting like he was going to break when I would have my hand down in front of him, I would just come right back on that dog's nose just to be sure he would sit there and not be creepin' out ahead of me. That helped a lot on that creepin'. Anyway, this was all done in training and some of those dogs had been whipped a time or two with those gloves.

"Anyway, I was at a field trial and an old judge down there in Texas, he said, 'Cotton, take those gloves off.' I said, 'Naaa, I got to keep 'em on.' He said, 'Cotton, take those gloves off, now. You're not going to place under me. I'm going to knock you out if you wear those gloves. I said, 'You can't do that – there ain't nothing in the rules about that!' He said, 'Cotton, take those gloves off.' I took 'em off and I won the field trial. But afterwards, I said, 'Now look, see these spots on my hands, that's skin cancer. Anyway, what do you think those gloves are going to make those dogs do?' He said, 'I'm not so dumb.' He wasn't either."

Cotton said he thought there were times, too, when the white gloves aided in handling, especially on long blind retrieves.

"On a real light day, I think a dog will see dark gloves better than he will white," Cotton said. "But white, against a bad background (such as a tree line), that's when you should wear white, where the dog can pick you or pick the movement up better than something dark that blends in. It's got to be a moving object too. You just put that hand out and say 'over,' and if he doesn't catch that hand going out and if you don't move that arm, hell, he might go the other way."

Cotton said Bakewell and he took "white" a little further.

"We used to wear white all the time, me and Bakewell," Cotton said. "He'd wear a white shirt and then he'd have raingear underneath that if he needed it. They'd think, oh, he's crazy. But the dog could see him."

Now, a white jacket is standard handling attire for field trials.

Cotton discovered many such handling and training techniques through trial and error. And although Cotton's reputation as a dog man was second to none throughout his career, he was considered especially proficient at preparing a dog for a big field trial. Cotton said the only magic to his method was knowing the dogs. What did that dog need to make him ready? Did he need to be built up? Taken down a notch?

"If you've got a big, high-rollin' dog, stretch him out on some singles. I think singles at a trial, right before you go, are very good for a dog," Cotton said. "I'm a great believer in that, especially if you've got a kind of high-goin' dog. It'll make a dog mark that first bird down. A lot of dogs are switchin' off too quick anyway (as the birds are shot, not concentrating on each fall). Maybe a hundred yards or a hundred and twenty-five. If nothing else, make 'em do the marks two or three times, just something to get the edge off of 'em.

"Maybe, if he was a little high or kind of had the urge to break, maybe throw one up in the air and crack his butt and not let him get it. Put him up. All the dogs are so different. You have to kind of know your dog. But I'm death on that single.

159

"When I won the '52 national at Weldon Springs, I worked that King Buck every morning on the way over. I worked him sometimes when it was so dark you couldn't hardly see him out there on a long single. I would give him two or three, depending on how he was rolling. They were pheasants. They weren't dummies. Sometimes they were shot and sometimes they were dead. It depended on if he was high or not. If he was a little too high, I shot 'em or had a man shoot 'em, and if I thought he was going to have a little tendency to leave, I'd crop him and he never got it, another dog did."

Cotton said another thing to avoid before a trial are cornfields, especially when the ground is frozen.

"You run a dog when it's really hard, frozen, real cold," Cotton said. "Those cornstalks are just like running into sticks. Even when they're not frozen, they're hard on a dog, on his front shoulders. You never want to run a dog in a cornfield before a trial. Keep that dog out of there because you'll get him sore and slow him down.

"Another thing I never did was drive into a trial twenty-five or thirty minutes before it was supposed to start and put that dog down. He hasn't had his feet on the ground. When you go to a place like that and you're going to run, get there at least an hour and a half or two hours ahead and get that dog out and walk him. Let him get that area under his feet. I don't mean run him all over, but maybe give him a single and just get him kind of acclimated. Just like you. When you ride a long way on a trip, when you get out, you're just not really sound on your feet. It takes you awhile to get organized. Dog's the same way."

All afternoon, Cotton had talked his talk. The group had listened like the pupils they were. And Cotton, never one to play the role of Infallible Professional for long, shifted gears on them. There were, he said, memorable screw-ups.

"I've sent 'em where I thought the blind was and it wasn't there. Once, I was handling a dog all over and the judge finally tapped me on the shoulder. 'Cotton, third tree from that one on the right is the blind.' 'Yes sir,' I said, 'toot...over.' It was Shed, Shed of Arden. Hell, they dropped me. But, man, he was handlin'.

"We used to have to go up and watch the blind put out then you had to go back and get your dog and then you came up and did the blind. You go up into a bunch of damn pine trees, and it's rough.

"And I used to locate my birds on marking tests sometimes by cattle out in the field. Mark my marked birds, you know. Cattle don't stay in one place all the time, they move. I've messed up like that before, too. I've had everything in a field trial happen to me sometime or other.

"I was up there in Wisconsin, running a field trial and this dog was out there rolling in cow pies. Heavy cover. I could see his tail now and then so I told the judge I thought he was takin' a runner. He said, "Well, let him work a little bit more.' Boy, that tail was gettin' in and finally I guess he got tired of rolling in that cow stuff so here he comes with the bird. Well, as luck would have it, the bird was still alive. So, boy, I made a big show – I got him by the neck and held it so that he started floppin' those wings, to make sure the judges could see it. Then I wrung its neck. I got second with that dog and he had cow manure all over him.

"Another time, this golden I was running got away out of sight on this river, chasing a duck that got caught in the current. Boy, I just knew he wouldn't come back without that bird. And pretty soon, here he comes up the bank. And what do you think he had? A chicken! A big ol' white hen he found down there somewhere. I just handed it to the judge, said thank-you, and got back to the truck and out of there as quick as I could. I got one on his owner, though, a real nice old man. Name was George Holmes. I said, 'Mr. Holmes, I didn't think you'd mind me lettin' him do that.' I mean things were tough back in those days. Anyway, I said, 'I didn't think you'd mind lettin' me get a chicken once in awhile with him.' He said, 'Well, Cotton, why don't you give him a pheasant or two before a trial anyway?' He thought I really did it on purpose."

The thought of Cotton Pershall standing on a riverbank with a big golden sitting beside him, tail wagging, holding a live chicken brought the house down. Which, Cotton said, is exactly what happened in the gallery at the field trial.

There are great memories, great old stories etched in Cotton's psyche. Some are dramatic, some sad, some funny, and more than a few perplexing. Such were the memories he conjured up about hip dysplasia and John Olin's efforts to cure the degenerative disease. Hip dysplasia is defined as an abnormal development of the hip joint in which the socket is less concave and more shallow than normal. This abnormality lowers efficient operation of the hip and often leads to ailments such as arthritis and related problems.

"We experimented on that hip dysplasia for quite a few years," Cotton said. "Mr. Olin put a lot of money into it – millions I guess. He had a specialist from Sweden over here. He spent a fortune.

"We worked a lot through Cornell University on other diseases in dogs, too. Cornell had the only, I guess, the only disease-free kennel. When you went in this building, well, you had to take a bath and put on their clothes and when you left, you took their clothes off, put your own clothes back on. We eventually had that up at Nilo. When we had dogs that had encephalitis or distemper, we'd centrifuge the blood and send it and the head back there. We had one dog that was never immunized against distemper and he lived to be about nine years old or so. He was a carrier, but he was always immune to getting it. All in all, this stuff, the immunizations, were developed with a lot of help from Mr. Olin.

"We tried to work with dysplasia. We did everything on that. We bred normal to normal, we'd get half (dysplastic). We bred dysplastic to normal, you might get a third. We bred dysplastic to dysplastic and got over half normal. You don't know how much work I did on that. Well, they thought, they're getting too much exercise. We built little square boxes and we put dogs in them. Then they thought the dogs were getting too heavy, so we almost starved them. Still they'd show dysplasia. There was work being done on greyhounds, too. And they quit showing dysplasia because when they started running 'em and when one couldn't run, they put him down. But you're worst breed of all, I guess, was your German shepherds. That was awful. And they're supposed to be a workin' dog. Scale walls and all that stuff. But they've just bred 'em and bred 'em. I can damn near tell whether a dog is dysplastic or not, I've seen so many of them.

"Mr. Olin spent so much time and money on trying to get rid of dysplasia and here you got people out there that just don't care. There were some great dogs that were dysplastic and people just bred 'em and bred 'em. Don't misunderstand me, you're going to get sound ones, good sound ones. But you're going to get a lot of dysplastic, too.

"And there's no such thing as one, two, three grades of dysplasia. If he's dysplastic, he's dysplastic. You take young puppies, before they get up to four months old. Take 'em out and hike 'em hard. You watch. A pup that lags back with those legs up under him a little bit, when they start with that, with those back legs almost straight under their hips, hoppin'. Well, then, you'd better watch out, 'cause they don't have any coordination with those joints.

"And the exercise thing. Hard work might make dysplasia come on quicker, but then it might strengthen the muscles around the hips and hold it back. You never know how it's going to affect individual dogs."

One member of the little group in Cotton's yard had, just a few months before, euthanized a nine-month-old puppy that was so dysplastic he could barely make the six-inch step to get into his kennel. The dog was out of a field champion sire and a bitch that was out of a field champion.

The group was silent. Cotton looked across the pasture behind his house where his registered Angus cattle stood in dramatic contrast against lush fescue.

The long shadows touched them and they lowed to Cotton to be fed.

Tableware was collected, car doors opened and closed, and goodbye's were said. Finally only one remained.

"Bob," Cotton said. "If you ever decide to write that book we've been talking about, be sure you write what Tony Berger told his boy, Phil."

"What was that, Cotton?"

"He said, 'watch Cotton all the time. But don't do what he says, do what he does.' Guess I'm not too good with words and I wouldn't want to tell something that wasn't right."

You're good enough, Cotton, with words that is.

"You know," Cotton sighed. "There wouldn't be anything that would make me happier right now than puttin' down about four good ones and dropping back about thirty or forty years."

He turned, waving, toward his pickup to take care of his evening chores. At 75, he was still burly, a strong man. But his steps were shorter and slower. There were only so many left.

I pulled my truck away from the kennel yard. I hadn't even closed the gate, and already I missed him.

GLOSSARY
OF
TERMS

Amateur field champion – A retriever that accumulates 10 points in open all-age stakes while handled by an amateur or 15 points in amateur all-age stakes, including a "win" (five points), earns the title "amateur field champion." On pedigrees, this is signified by the letters AFC preceding the dog's name. A dog that has earned both his field championship and his amateur field championship is recognized on pedigrees by the prefix "FC-AFC."

Balk or "no go" – A "no go" is a no-no. This means the dog has been given the command to retrieve and refused to go.

Baseball drill – A handling drill in which the dog sits at the pitcher's mound and bumpers are thrown to first base, second base, and third base. The handler stands at home plate and casts the dog to various "bases."

Blind retrieve – In hunting situations, a dog often misses the fall of a bird. In retrieving a bird that he has not seen fall, the dog is sent "blind." A blind retrieve involves a dog running a "line," given by the handler, and responding to whistle and hand signals. For training purposes, blind retrieves are broken down into "water blinds" and "land blinds."

Break – A dog that leaves his handler's side before a command to retrieve is given is said to "break."

Cast – A directional signal given by a handler.

Cheat – A field trial term. A dog that runs the shoreline instead of taking a direct line through the water to a mark has "cheated."

Cold blind – A blind retrieve on which the dog has not been trained.

Diversion – A distraction for the dog. Often, in a field trial, marks and blind retrieves are run in the same area. If the dog picks up the marks first, they are considered "diversions" for the blind.

Electronic collar – A training device involving an electronic receiver that is attached to a collar worn by the dog and a remote transmitter that is operated by the trainer. The trainer activates the collar by pressing a button or buttons on the transmitter.

Field champion – A retriever that accumulates 10 points in open all age stakes, including a "win" (five points), earns the title "field champion." On pedigrees, this is signified by the letters FC preceding a dog's name.

Field & Stream Trophy – An annual award, once given to the retriever who accumulated the most points in open all-age stakes during the course of a calendar year. Although the national retriever club still recognizes the high point dogs in both amateur and open all-age stakes, the Field & Stream Trophy is no longer awarded.

Field trial – Competition in which retrievers are tested in various capacities. Field trials that are licensed by the American Kennel Club award points toward the titles of field champion and amateur field champion. A field trial is divided into the following categories:

The derby – a stake for dogs between six months and two years of age. Derby tests deal strictly with marking, usually singles and doubles and in some cases triples.

The qualifying – entrants are generally tested on multiple marks and blind retrieves on both land and water. This stake is viewed as a level between the derby and the all-age stakes.

The open all-age – this stake is the top level. Tests consist of multiple marks, sometimes quads, multiple blind retrieves, and so on. The open all-age is the realm of the professional handler.

The amateur all-age – basically the same stake as the Open All-Age. The major difference involves the handlers. Only amateur handlers may enter this stake.

Finished retriever – A dog that is consistently successful on multiple marked retrieves on both land and water, and blind retrieves on both land and water.

Flyer – A live bird, generally a duck, pheasant, or pigeon, that is thrown and shot for the dog to retrieve. A "flyer" is shot by gunners in the field during training or field trials.

Force training – When a dog is forced to perform a task through pressure by the trainer.

Freezing – This, too, is a field trial term used to describe the circumstance in which a dog returns from a retrieve and will not give up a bird.

"Fun" trial – A field trial that is not licensed or sanctioned by the American Kennel Club. Retriever clubs generally hold at least one "fun" trial (often called a "club" trial) per year.

Gunners – A term used to describe the people who shoot and/or throw birds at a field trial or during a training session.

Handler-thrown marks – Bumpers or birds that are thrown by the handler for the dog to retrieve. Generally speaking, the simplest form of a marked retrieve.

Handling – When a dog will sit on a single whistle blast and obey directional casts by his handler, the dog is "handling."

Hardmouth – A dog that renders his birds unfit for the table. As a general rule, the dog should not break the skin on a bird.

Hip dysplasia – An abnormal development of the hip joint in which the socket is less concave and more shallow than normal. Dysplasia often shows up under physical exertion.

Honor – If two dogs are working and one is sent to retrieve, the remaining dog is expected to sit and "honor" the working dog.

Line or lining – When a dog is sent to retrieve, he runs a "line" to the bird or bumper. A good line is a straight line, directly through cover, ditches, etc. A bad line means the dog avoided the obstacles.

Marks – These are bumpers or birds that the dog sees fall. Marks are separated into two categories – water marks and land marks. Further distinctions involve the number of birds that a dog must "mark."

Single mark: the dog is expected to retrieve one bird, usually thrown by a gunner in the field.

Double mark: the dog is expected to watch two birds fall before he is released to retrieve. The dog generally retrieves the last bird down first. The first bird that falls becomes a "memory bird," the location of which must be remembered by the dog.

Triple mark: This is generally considered "all-age" work. Three birds are thrown, two of which are "memory birds."

Memory bird – A marked retrieve that the dog must remember. The second bird to be picked up on a double retrieve.

Memory blind – A memory blind is a blind retrieve that the dog knows, usually created through repetition of a sight blind.

National Champion – There are two national championship stakes for field trial retrievers in the United States. The National Open is held in November. This stake is run by both professionals and amateurs. To qualify, a dog must win an "open" stake and accumulate at least two more open all-age points prior to the running of the national stake. The National Amateur Championship Stake is held in June. As the name implies, only amateur handlers may qualify and compete in this stake. To qualify, a dog, handled by an amateur, must win an amateur all-age stake or an open all-age stake and accumulate at least two more all-age points prior to the running of the National Amateur stake.

Old fall – An old fall is the area of a mark that the dog already has retrieved. A dog is said to have an "old fall" problem if, when working on multiple marks, he persists in returning to previously retrieved marks or "old falls."

Pop – A pop occurs when a retriever is sent to retrieve, either on a "blind" or a "mark," and he stops, without hearing or seeing a command, sits, and faces the handler. This indicates that the dog is not confident about the retrieve. Popping on "marks" often occurs when a trainer concentrates too hard on handling. The dog is so accustomed to the trainer helping him find the birds that he no longer hunts on his own.

Runner – A "flyer" that is not cleanly killed and proceeds to walk or run away from the area of the fall.

Salted mark – This is a training exercise which should build confidence in young dogs. A bird thrower drops several bumpers or birds in an area. He then stands away from the area and, upon the signal from the handler, throws a mark into the "salted" area. This enables the pup to be successful on the marked retrieve and prevents a lengthy hunt.

Sight blind – A training term. A "sight blind" may be established in a variety of ways. Usually, though, a sight blind is created by laying several bumpers in a pile, then throwing a bumper the dog can see to the pile. The dog picks the first bumper up as a "mark." When sent back to the pile a second time, without the aid of the "mark," the dog is running a "sight blind."

Steady – A retriever is said to be steady when he will sit by his handler's side and wait for the "retrieve" command while birds are being shot in front of him.

Switch bird – A bird that is shot while the dog is returning with a mark. Sometimes the dog will drop the bird he is carrying and pick up the freshly shot bird. This is called a "switch."

Three-legged pattern – Three sight "blinds," run from the same starting point, that are used for "lining" and "handling" practice. The blinds become a "pattern" for the dog through repetition. He picks up first the right leg of the pattern, then the middle leg, and finally the left leg – thus a "pattern." When the dog has learned the pattern, the handler should be able to line the dog indiscriminately down the leg of his choice.

Whistle sit – Most retrievers are taught to "sit" on a single whistle blast. The whistle, in this case, takes the place of the handler's vocal command to sit. A dog must be thoroughly trained on the "whistle sit" if he is to become proficient at "handling."